More praise for *Stacking the Deck*

"Some leaders drive the train and some are out in front of the engine laying new track. The real differences are made by those who imagine new ways of transport and inspire others to create them. What's most exciting about *Stacking the Deck* is that it comes from an operator, as Dave Pottruck has a lifetime of experience in the excitement, disappointment, and elation inherent in radically changing the order of things. This is a practical guide to bold change—one to use immediately and often."

—Terry Pearce, founder and president, Leadership Communication

"Dave Pottruck's book is packed with good advice, clear thinking, and a well-organized blueprint for anyone who intends to embark on leading change. His passion for leading change and his expertise as a mentor and a leader come through loud and clear, making *Stacking the Deck* an educational and compelling read."

—Elliot Weissbluth, CEO, HighTower Advisors

"Being an entrepreneur isn't a profession. It's a condition or maybe an incurable disease. I'd say the same thing about being an agent of organizational change. Both rest on a belief that anything we're doing today, we can do better tomorrow—if we have skills and tenacity. Dave Pottruck, who's been there and done that, points readers in the right direction."

—Howard Tullman, CEO, 1871

"Many books have been written about why organizations need to change, yet leading change remains one of the hardest things leaders do. *Stacking the Deck* is the first practical, step-by-step guide to leading transformational or breakthrough change. I wish Dave Pottruck had written this book before I was turning around drugstore.com—and you can be sure I'll keep it as a reference!"

—Dawn Lepore, advisor and consultant; board member, AOL, Coupons.com, and Real Networks, Inc.; former CEO and chairman, drugstore.com

"We've all learned the following truth the hard way: managing change is hard! Leaders need a practical guide to achieve breakthrough transformation—and this is exactly what Dave Pottruck provides in *Stacking the Deck*. He's been in the trenches and knows what it takes to successfully lead the change process and create an ongoing innovation culture for your organization."

—Patrick T. Harker, president, University of Delaware

"*Stacking the Deck* is not just about leading business transformation. It's also about the transformation of a business leader. Dave Pottruck shares his deeply personal journey and those of other seasoned executives as they navigate leading change in uncharted territory. By outlining the do's and don'ts, Pottruck's guidebook equips every C-level executive with the leadership courage and the framework for success in tackling today's exponential and continuous challenges."

—Lauren Doliva, global managing partner, chief advisor network,
Heidrick & Struggles

"I am fortunate to work for an organization with a very focused mission—sustained competitive excellence at the Olympic and Paralympic Games. The complicated part of our business is not deciding what to do, but rather how to do it. How do you make changes in a constituent-based organization where the constituents have equal passion but very different objectives and abilities? It is almost as if Dave Pottruck's book was written with us in mind. As practical as it is thoughtful, this is a must-read if you recognize the need for change but don't know where to start."

—Scott Blackmun, CEO, United States Olympic and Paralympic Committee

"Where others see challenges and problems, Dave Pottruck sees opportunities. Throughout my time with Dave at Charles Schwab, he sought out transformational change with greater and lesser success but always with an eye to opportunity. Dave moderates the complexity of change through simplified checklists and gives you confidence that you, too, can implement radical change."

—Jan Hier-King, cofounder, Bicycle Financial; former CIO
and head of human resources, Charles Schwab

"There's great comfort in knowing even the best leaders and the best plans run into resistance. Dave Pottruck's detailed, step-by-step guidance for overcoming barriers and leading change successfully is both practical and inspiring, whether you're in the profit or not-for-profit world. I'll put the insights and wisdom of *Stacking the Deck* to good use!"

—John Denniston, president, St. Vincent de Paul Society, San Mateo County;
former partner, Kleiner Perkins

"Attempting to lead breakthrough change without this book is like bringing a knife to a gunfight. Who wouldn't want to gain an unfair advantage by tapping into Dave Pottruck's vast experience and powerful, purposeful approach, augmented with valuable insights from other successful leaders? *Stacking the Deck* will help you succeed."

—Jim Hornthal, chairman and cofounder, Zignal Labs and LaunchPad Central

STACKING
THE DECK

STACKING THE DECK

HOW TO LEAD BREAKTHROUGH CHANGE AGAINST ANY ODDS

David S. Pottruck

Foreword by
Tony La Russa

JB JOSSEY-BASS™
A Wiley Brand

Published by Jossey-Bass
A Wiley Brand
One Montgomery Street, Suite 1200, San Francisco, CA 94104-4594—www.josseybass.com

Jossey-Bass books and products are available through most bookstores. To contact Jossey-Bass directly call our Customer Care Department within the U.S. at 800-956-7739, outside the U.S. at 317-572-3986, or fax 317-572-4002.

Wiley publishes in a variety of print and electronic formats and by print-on-demand. Some material included with standard print versions of this book may not be included in e-books or in print-on-demand. If this book refers to media such as a CD or DVD that is not included in the version you purchased, you may download this material at **http://booksupport.wiley.com**. For more information about Wiley products, visit **www.wiley.com**.

Library of Congress Cataloging-in-Publication Data

Pottruck, David S., 1948-
  Stacking the deck : how to lead breakthrough change against any odds / David S. Pottruck.
    1 online resource.
  Includes index.
  Description based on print version record and CIP data provided by publisher; resource not viewed.
  ISBN 978-1-118-96689-1 (pdf)—ISBN 978-1-118-96690-7 (epub)—ISBN 978-1-118-96688-4 (hardback) 1. Organizational change. 2. Business planning. 3.Management. I. Title.
  HD58.8
  658.4′06—dc23

                                                                                2014023069

Printed in the United States of America
FIRST EDITION
HB Printing   10 9 8 7 6 5 4 3 2 1

To my grandchildren,
Max, Roxanne, Charlotte, Harriet, and Leo
With hopes for successful breakthrough changes and a better
world for all of us

CONTENTS

Foreword by Tony La Russa   xi

Introduction   1

PART ONE THE STACKING THE DECK PROCESS

1   Step One: Establishing the Need to Change
and a Sense of Urgency   15

2   Step Two: Assembling and Unifying Your
Leadership Team   31

3   Step Three: Developing and Communicating
a Clear and Compelling Vision of the Future   46

4   Step Four: Planning Ahead for Known and
Unknown Barriers   58

5   Step Five: Creating a Workable Plan   72

6   Step Six: Partitioning the Project and Building
Momentum with Early Wins   88

7   Step Seven: Defining Metrics, Developing
Analytics, and Communicating Results   99

8   Step Eight: Assessing, Recruiting, and
       Empowering the Broader Team   116
9   Step Nine: Testing with Pilots to Increase Success   134

PART TWO LEADING THE CHANGE

10 Using the Nine Steps to Bring Your Initiative
       to the Real World   153
11 Communicating and Connecting to Inspire   170
12 Innovation: Ideas and Perspectives   194

Epilogue: Final Comments and Reflections   207
Appendix: Featured Leaders   214
Acknowledgments   221
About the Author   224
Index   227

FOREWORD

By Tony La Russa

When you imagine breakthrough change, does baseball come to mind? Probably only on a limited basis, since baseball is often thought of as a traditional game, changing little over time. That may still be true in Little League and high school, but in the major leagues, baseball has changed dramatically, on the field, behind the scenes, and in the front office.

Baseball has been part of my life for over fifty years. I started playing professionally when I was seventeen and I've been a major league manager for more than three decades. Over those years, I've seen Major League Baseball embrace change while retaining its traditional roots, on and off the field. MLB Commissioner Bud Selig has never been afraid to innovate, even in a game that traditionally has been resistant to change. He recently tapped a few of us with uniform experience to join with MLB staff to see if we could bring the benefits of technology to enhanced instant replay in baseball without slowing down the pace of the game. Could we build a model that worked, that didn't stop every play, but could help in instances in which human error had the potential to dramatically change the outcome of the competition?

This was a radical idea for baseball and a very public change. Being able to identify and clarify possible kinks in advance—to test the concept before rolling it out—was critical. We ran field tests during fall development games and spring training, where we could acquaint umpires and uniform personnel with the enhanced replay system. With these tests behind us and with the addition of two new crews of umpires, we have seen how replay challenges, very selectively used, can improve both the reality and the perception that the right call was made. The process has proven just how difficult the umpires' jobs are—and how good they are.

For this change, we had the advantage of time for extended advance planning, testing, and risk management. We also had an exceptional staff manning the entire effort. But what if you don't have these advantages? Then you will have to rely on the depth of your experience and perhaps outside advisors to spell the difference between success and failure. And now, you can also rely on the accumulated experiences of Dave Pottruck and the dozen top leaders he interviewed in developing and testing the concepts that appear in *Stacking the Deck*. His book provides the benefits of a range and depth of experience in leading breakthrough change that would take many lifetimes to accrue.

About a month before Dave asked me to consider writing this foreword, I'd taken on a new position, one that was new to me and to all of baseball: chief baseball officer of the Arizona Diamondbacks. The team had been struggling and the front office realized it was time for breakthrough change. It's no secret that struggles create great opportunities. Sometimes that's hard to see from the inside, but the concept is clear to Dave. *Stacking the Deck* helps readers discover the opportunities that obstacles hold. That next step—leading breakthrough changes that turn opportunities into success—is one that all leaders must face, whether on the ball field, behind a desk, or in the boardroom.

Although my position is unique in the baseball world, its functions are familiar to many businesses. I was hired to evaluate and inspire people, and to help make our organization's teams more competitive by some changes in how we play the game. These are not easy tasks under any circumstances. But in baseball, the product has more moving parts than in most businesses: it's the team at large, the players for each game, the end result, the fan base, the league standing. Ultimately, the goal is a championship team and a winning season. And—in contrast to a tangible product off a production line—each year the product we're aiming for resets. We restart at zero, and are always competing against the changing rosters of 29 other teams.

On paper, I'm responsible to the organization and the people who hired me; personally, I'm also responsible to the members of the team, all the people involved with the team, and all the fans. My focus, as always, is very much about working with people. Success requires developing personal relationships. It's about communicating and inspiring people throughout the organization to be and perform at their best. Most particularly, in this new position, it's about inspiring players to be professional ball players and contributing teammates while also providing them the fundamental tools to succeed.

We are face to face with the effects of two of the major changes in baseball (and professional sports in general): the distortions in basic values and the distractions of fame and fortune that come along with the contracts today's players receive. Another dramatic change stems from the influence of analytics and metrics that can now be captured to help improve the product. Helpful as these numbers are in calculating averages and setting the teams, players are human and analytics alone are no substitute for human judgment and experience.

If you created teams by the numbers alone, as people do in fantasy baseball, putting together the best team for each game might seem simple. But, critical as they are, the historic numbers—players' batting averages against certain pitchers, base-running speed, steals—and the newly created analytic measures cannot reliably predict future performance. Once the teams are on the field, the human element trumps the metrics every time. It's the unmeasurable factors of competitive heart, toughness, and the willingness and ability to be a team member and a team player that give the edge. It's understanding the glories of competition and preparing the best you can. It's feeling the urgency and passion, and stepping up individually and as a cohesive team that make the difference—in each moment and in each game.

When it's all working right, the long-range goal of a winning season comes closer, game by game. But professional baseball is a long haul: 162 games over six months tells only part of the story. Tenacity, persistence, and resilience are all absolute requirements. There's the travel, the training, the injuries, the losses, the absence from loved ones. Years ago, when I was considering whether to continue as a coach or a manager, the late, great Cardinals' coach George Kissell told me that I had to have the desire and then asked, "Do you love the game? Do you want to learn it?" It was a simple formula that made clear his point that unless you relish learning every aspect of the game, you're not cut out for coaching or managing.

His advice really resonated and is, in my opinion, relevant for anyone heading for a baseball career. More broadly, his formula is applicable in approaching any field, determining whether you are sincerely passionate about it and can put your heart into it. You simply have to love your field and learn it in detail; you need passion, enthusiasm, and skills; and you must be personally accountable to be successful and to stay in the game.

No matter what you're involved with or what you're leading, if you love it, the fact that staying ahead is a constant learning experience becomes a pleasure. You must also learn to be a leader and to demonstrate that you are worthy of trust and respect. Every single day. Only then can you perform your leadership duties and reach your goals.

In baseball, we prepare for success by looking ahead, knowing the competition, lining up our players to be their best possible fit, and competing at our highest level for the winning score. Similarly, throughout the nine-step process set forth in *Stacking the Deck*, Dave shows how experienced and maturing leaders can develop a game plan for success and be better prepared as they approach and then overcome the challenges of breakthrough change. He demonstrates the importance of communicating honestly and effectively, in ways that keep the urgency and the importance of the change foremost—and in ways that move individuals and the organization into a better future.

He demonstrates the importance of caring about your people, not just on a professional level but on a personal level. Further, with his emphasis on linking the purpose and the mission and helping people see the reasons—the *why* behind the changes—Dave gets to the heart of important undercurrents in today's world.

There's no crystal ball to tell you with certainty how quickly you can get to your goals, but the process Dave sets forth provides signposts and guidance that you can use to increase your chances for success. Whether in baseball or in a more traditional business, getting people to believe and having them be all in with the vision and the goals are crucial. You must constantly work to build a strong culture supported on a foundation of trust. That foundation, plus the leadership lessons and process structure provided by *Stacking the Deck* will enable you to achieve breakthrough change and breakthrough success more efficiently and with fewer detours. This is not to say it's easy. Achieving excellence is hard work that demands nonstop and unrelenting effort. It's also how lasting value gets created.

STACKING
THE DECK

INTRODUCTION

We are continually faced with a series of great opportunities brilliantly disguised as insolvable problems.
— John W. Gardner Secretary of Health, Education and Welfare under
Lyndon Johnson

One reality of business that seasoned executives know well—often by learning it the hard way—is that introducing and implementing breakthrough change is an uphill battle. No matter how necessary the change or how seemingly evident the need, this process demands continuous hard work. This book is designed to help you understand and overcome the difficulties in finding and advancing a smoother path.

The problems leaders face are perhaps more pervasive today, given the accelerated pace of business in a much flatter world. However, problems also present opportunities. You can learn to recognize such opportunities and show others that the potential victories far outweigh the discomfort that change will elicit.

Breakthrough change refers to those disruptive initiatives that dramatically, profoundly affect the organization and the people in it.

It redefines the prospects for the future and interrupts the organization's cautious momentum plan with incremental improvement. Breakthrough change can increase revenues or reduce costs. It can mean a new distribution channel or a new line of products. And it can be as exciting as launching an international expansion or as scary as a massive restructuring and downsizing effort. Breakthrough change also depends on the situation, or context. What is breakthrough to one organization can be business as usual to another.

You need to do everything you can to stack the deck in favor of success. That's exactly what you'll learn how to do in this book.

WHY "STACKING THE DECK"?

I never intended to write this book. But as it turned out, there were no practical books on change written by and for people from midcareer managers to global senior executives. There was no resource for on-the-ground leaders seeking clear ways to develop the skills to implement change within their organizations, whether for-profit or nonprofit. Plenty of books and articles about leading or managing change have been written, many of them very insightful. Some, especially John Kotter's groundbreaking *Leading Change*, have stood the test of time and are invaluable. But none of them offered the whole picture, or at least not the picture that I saw through the lens of my background and experience—the practical, operational side of leading breakthrough, transformational change. And none of them deeply engaged with the human reality of leading big, risky change initiatives—not in ways that could be immediately put to use.

I saw a need for a book that would go beyond outlining the strategies and processes required for success, one that would also address the challenges leaders are likely to confront in driving and implementing change. A book that told in-the-trenches stories of individuals who led bold, sweeping change; that walked readers through the social and emotional reality of leading others without shortchanging the real difficulties involved in promoting a change to people who, perhaps rightly, are fearful of it. A book not for the novice, but for people who have years of firsthand experience leading others.

These are the people I teach in various venues, ranging from Wharton's Executive MBA program through corporate programs tailored for specific needs. Whether as emerging executives or seasoned senior executives, these leaders have high expectations and enormous demands on their time. In all of my classes and presentations I offer a specific nine-step Stacking the Deck process and an approach to leadership that students and participants may never have encountered before, either in their careers or in their formal business education. By exploring leadership within the framework of a problem to be solved, this approach enables people to better understand the demands and requirements of leadership. It enables them to look at the whole picture: the people they must lead, the purpose of the change, the steps through which they must travel, and the actual situations they will confront. There's nothing abstract about change when it affects the job security, 401(k) programs, and even identities of real people in an organization. This process of contextualizing leadership strikes a chord and makes the information real, current, and immediately useful.

Eventually I realized that the book I was looking for would have to come from someone like me—someone with a personal history of business leadership that has provided a wealth of practical, hands-on lessons. Someone who had to learn on the ground, and who sometimes made big mistakes. Someone whose many attempts to lead breakthrough change were much more difficult than they actually had to be—but were certainly more instructive as a result. Someone who could keep you from making those same mistakes.

STACKING THE DECK FOR BREAKTHROUGH CHANGE

Most organizations' processes and culture are structured for predictability, reliability, control, and risk minimization. Breakthrough change is the polar opposite. It is unpredictable and favors responsiveness to new realities over control and staying the course. Breakthrough change is inherently risky and goes against every instinct the leaders of the company have developed over the course of their careers. Is it any wonder, then, that employees often resist breakthrough change—even in companies whose leaders say it's exactly what they need?

Every business is filled with people who depend heavily on procedures continuing "as they have always been." That's what "expertise" is; you spend 10, 15, or even 20 years doing something a certain way and therefore become an expert in it. Your knowledge of the way things have always been done is what gives you value as an employee. So when some brand-new executive comes in and tells you everything is about to change—but it's going to be great and you should greet it with open arms—how would you feel?

If you answered "pretty darn nervous," you're not alone, or irrational. People's emotional responses to a specific change initiative can be unpredictable and very powerful. Leaders must find ways to help people see the need for change and then inspire them to move toward it with confidence and urgency. This is a daunting struggle and one that is not explored deeply enough in most books on leading or managing change. *Stacking the Deck* explains not just the *what* of change but the *how*.

The nine-step Stacking the Deck process is designed to mitigate the risks that come with change by having you take concrete steps to increase your chances of success. This preparation does not make the change less bold—and it doesn't guarantee success. What it does do is create an advantage (or more accurately, a series of advantages). These steps—culled from my experience, tested in practice, shared, and refined—provide a guide to preparing and planning so that your change initiative, and your team, have the best possible shot at succeeding. The Stacking the Deck process allows you to take on big, transformative change with increasing confidence and momentum because you know that you have a proven approach going in.

I've seen successes and I've seen failures. The failures were not because the proposed change was toxic or wrongheaded, and not because the effort was inadequate. Instead, these failures were often rooted in an inadequate understanding of how truly difficult it is to overcome resistance, to deal with uncertainty, to respond to new facts, and to execute the myriad details necessary for success.

You may know the phrase "stacking the deck" to mean preparing a deck of playing cards so that you will almost certainly win the game rather than rely on chance. This is what I was thinking of when I coined the phrase in reference to leading breakthrough change—except that the Stacking the Deck process is not designed to cheat other players. It implies instead that thinking through and preparing for all the steps and processes we will need to undertake vastly increases our chances of success.

Stacking the Deck distills the useful techniques and processes I have learned throughout my career into a series of logical and sequential steps for leading breakthrough change. Understanding and following these steps—and reading about my own experiences and those of the leaders I've interviewed—will enable you to avoid many decades of trial-and-error that we have worked through. You will learn practical, relevant ways to deal with change and succeed, without experiencing the risks and the mistakes that were required to amass this knowledge.

A GUIDE TO *STACKING THE DECK*

The book is divided into two parts. Part One describes the Stacking the Deck process, nine steps through which nearly every breakthrough change inevitably goes. They're presented in the order in which you should undertake them, though there are exceptions. The steps often overlap, and circumstances frequently demand that you double back to repeat or redo a previous step in the process. Change is not linear and nothing about this should throw you off your game plan.

1. Step One is *establishing the need to change and creating a sense of urgency* around that need. Not only is this step critical—it's critically positioned. Much of the Stacking the Deck process focuses on the psychological aspects of change. Making the change necessary and urgent in the minds of those most affected by it is the social and emotional foundation for everything that comes afterward.

2. Step Two focuses on *recruiting and unifying your inner team* of innovation leaders who will help you define the future and make it a reality.

3. Step Three requires that you *develop and communicate a clear and compelling vision* of the future. This is the task that your new innovation leadership team must own.

4. Step Four enables you to anticipate, understand, and plan to *overcome potential barriers to success*. Some will always surprise you—but you can plan to deal with the ones you can anticipate.

5. Step Five describes how to *develop a clear, executable plan* that answers all the big questions a given change poses, while still recognizing the uncertainty and risk involved with undertakings of this magnitude.

6. Step Six explains how to *break the change initiative into manageable pieces* to build momentum and exponentially increase your chances of success.

7. Step Seven discusses *defining metrics, developing analytics,* and the importance of actively *sharing your results,* posting them as motivational tools to further build momentum. The possibilities and opportunities presented by big data are discussed in relation to leading breakthrough change.

8. Step Eight builds on the earlier Step Two principles for building the inner team and addresses the need for *assessing, recruiting, and empowering the broader team.*

9. Step Nine covers the *power of pilot implementations* and the critical differences between proof-of-concept pilots and scalability pilots.

Together these nine steps represent a plan of action that will take you from the first realization that a change needs to be made through a complete shift in the way you implement this change. This process is a practical guide you can use as you initiate and lead the change process. The questions and action items at the end of each chapter in Part One are designed to guide you through the process and serve as a mental review whenever you are working through big transitions.

Part Two turns to the higher-order skills that are necessary for success in the process of leading breakthrough change. Chapter Ten describes the sequencing of the steps and provides practical advice on the final implementation and rollout process by which you bring the initiative to the real world. Chapter Eleven focuses on developing leadership communication skills and the ability to be more inspirational, both of which are foundational to the entire Stacking the Deck process. The final chapter and the epilogue look at innovation and change leadership in general.

A caveat: this book is not about how to *create* innovative ideas and strategies. Its purpose is to show you how to implement the transformative concept that is described within. *Stacking the Deck* provides a wealth of examples born of my own and others' experience, stories that are intended to help you bridge the gap between idea and reality as you lead change.

VOICES OF EXPERTS

As I began the serious business of writing a book, I naturally sought advice and counsel from business leaders who had led extraordinary change initiatives during their careers, people who had a range of relevant experience. I spoke with eBay CEO John Donahoe, former Amylin president and CEO Ginger Graham, former Wells Fargo CEO Dick Kovacevich, and Starbucks chief executive officer Howard Schultz—all experienced CEOs who have seen change from virtually every vantage point. I also wanted some newer leaders who had recently become CEOs or presidents. These interviewees included San Francisco Giants CEO Larry Baer, JetBlue CEO Dave Barger, Asurion CEO Steve Ellis, Pinkberry CEO Ron Graves, and Intel's president Renée James. Mike Bell, former member of the iPhone development team at Apple and now head of new mobile devices at Intel, and Debby Hopkins, Citicorp chief innovation officer, provide the perspective of senior executives who are directly leading bold change. And finally, to discuss the important skills needed for leadership communication, there is simply no one more knowledgeable and experienced than Terry Pearce, consultant and author of *Leading Out Loud*. Brief biographies for each of the interviewees are in the back of the book. More-detailed biographies, recommended readings relevant to the steps, readings on leadership communication, and supplemental material are available on the book's website.

This group of interviewees shared their experiences in large public companies and small private companies, from high tech to consumer products, retailing and services. Some of these organizations are recent or somewhat mature start-ups; others have been around for decades or even a century. One individual has spent his entire career in one company, and three others were or still are consultants who have seen bold projects succeed or fail at dozens of companies over their careers. The breadth of experiences represented by the leaders you will meet in *Stacking the Deck* gave the book the depth I was searching for.

These leaders expanded my thinking, challenged some of my initial ideas, and helped make my principles much more complete and robust. I have quoted them extensively throughout the book, and their influence and value go far beyond the specific quotes I've included. Simply stated, every part of this book benefited and was transformed by the lessons these incredible leaders provided. They provided validation of many of the ideas I had been teaching and added their own stories of how experiences unfolded for them. My hope is that by presenting parts of my history and that of other leaders, I can help readers leap over potential pitfalls on their own leadership paths, thus accelerating success, their own and that of their organizations.

HEADING INTO CHANGE

My experiences in a variety of capacities for corporations that differed in size, goals, industry, corporate culture, and more have shaped how I see change. A brief overview will give a better sense of where these principles came from and the opportunities I've had to put them into practice—or when I failed to put them into practice.

In 1976, I began my career in financial services at Citibank, where I had my first experiences in implementing breakthrough change initiatives. I went from Citi to Shearson, a traditional brokerage that was not interested in change; they were far more interested in sales. When I joined Charles Schwab in 1984, it was still a fairly small company. CEO Chuck Schwab and his chief operating officer, Larry Stupski, were never afraid to dream big. Chuck was the visionary guy and Larry was the strategist and implementation leader. His job was to sift through Chuck's myriad ideas, find the three most likely to work, and get them done. They were courageous leaders and I knew that I was indeed fortunate to join this team.

Originally hired as the director of marketing, I was working on small improvements in the types of ads we were running, the ways we were handling our inbound inquiries, and how we were measuring success. As my career grew, the changes become bolder and more challenging. Joining Schwab when I did was a huge stroke of luck: circumstances and corporate culture combined to provide an unprecedented space for experimentation and risk-taking. I made my first stabs at leading breakthrough change there, and I discovered a lot of ways I would lead differently in the future.

Since those early days, I have served on the boards of many companies—from companies in their earliest stages, to young public companies, to Fortune 50 corporations. I have seen them succeed, and I have seen them stumble and fail. I've been part of two start-ups that invested over $150 million in getting off the ground. One failed completely and the other is blossoming even as I write this. I've been on the board of Intel since 1998, and I've seen their successes and the challenges they've faced.

I have been on just about every side of change, big or small. I've seen and made many mistakes, sometimes of judgment and sometimes of process. Somewhere there may be a file of mistakes labeled, "What was Dave thinking?" The redeeming fact is I usually didn't make the same mistake twice. As a self-proclaimed change junkie, I kept at it, trying new ideas and tactics, and learning; over time, I started to succeed more and more.

CHANGE AND LEARNING ARE CONTINUOUS

Breakthrough change never, ever stops while the world progresses. Competition, the marketplace, and technological advances make it necessary to keep growing and changing. In my own career, I experienced firsthand what happens when you stop leading bold change. I weathered a number of storms during my two decades at Charles Schwab, but the burst of the dotcom bubble in the early 2000s caught me by surprise. Suddenly, my job as Schwab's CEO became entirely about finding new ways to downsize, new places to cut. I did what I had to do: I downsized a 25,000-person company by 10,000 people. But I was slow and uncertain, and had trouble coping with this new reality of my job. I was emotionally paralyzed by the prospect of waking up every day and thinking about the men and women—people I knew well and who had been instrumental in making the company successful—whose jobs would be eliminated. And it was my job to direct these firings, by the thousands.

I think the Schwab board could tell that my heart was not in it. And they could certainly tell that I had stopped scanning the horizon for breakthrough transformative change. I left the company in 2004 due to a combination of my own inability to continue innovating and my board's shrunken patience. Being fired was devastating, and is still painful to this day. Much as I wish I had responded to the downturn differently, Schwab needed more than I was able to deliver. I had stopped leading change, and instead I became a change that someone else needed to make.

I tell this story to make it very clear that the strategies and plans described in Stacking the Deck are not easy for me, or for anyone, to implement. Overcoming emotion (your own and others'), convincing people to follow you, maintaining an extraordinary level of tenacity and resilience, conceptualizing change, and realizing it successfully: these are all tremendously difficult. Every leader I interviewed emphasized the inherent difficulty of breakthrough change. Over and over, they told of struggles that tested people to their very core and how they persevered through grit and determination.

This book is not intended to convince you to make breakthrough changes. The world will convince you to do that! Instead, it is designed to help you make those necessary changes as effectively as possible.

LEADING BREAKTHROUGH CHANGE IS NOT FOR THE FAINT OF HEART

A fundamental truth lies at the core of introducing any large-scale change: leading change requires leading people. Any transformation you propose, small or large, will ultimately not succeed if you don't have the leadership skills to drive the process forward. Success never comes from one person's efforts; transformative change is a team sport. There is, therefore, an absolute requirement for exceptional leadership skills, a proven process, and a team capable of getting the job done. As a consequence, leadership and communication are constant threads throughout the Stacking the Deck process and throughout this book. In fact, I encourage you to be sure you have truly absorbed the information and guidance provided in the chapter on leadership communication (Chapter Eleven) before you begin to implement the steps. The time you spend on the foundational steps of preparing, planning, and communicating will definitely reap benefits.

Today's business world will always demand that you do it faster, spend less money, and still get exceptional results. The ongoing pressure to take shortcuts is likely to intensify in years to come. Sometimes you may have no choice but to compress the effort and consider skipping something—in fact, some changes do not require every step in the process. However, it's relatively easy to decide to cut corners when you're thinking abstractly; it's more difficult when you can actually see which elements you are cutting out and what they specifically contribute to ensuring success. Since the Stacking the Deck process concretely shows you all the steps of a change initiative from inception to completion, you can make needed cuts with an understanding of exactly what you are removing—and what the consequences will likely be. Each of the nine steps will guide you along the way to breakthrough change.

But make no mistake: leading breakthrough change is definitely not for the faint of heart. In fact, I found it rather heartening that time and again, the people I interviewed—leaders across all fields in businesses around the world—reinforced just how much more difficult leading breakthrough change is than anyone anticipates.

More than money, time, or resources, it's your ability to lead people, your tenacity, and your grit that will determine your ultimate success or failure. Before communicating about the change, be sure you fully understand what the change represents to all of the groups who will be involved. If you remain open to possibilities, eager for constant challenges, and lucky enough to find mentors, your path will be easier. Most important, understand that inspirational leadership communication is critical to each step along the way, every single day.

PART ONE

THE STACKING THE DECK PROCESS

Breakthrough change is inherently unpredictable, making failures inevitable and flexibility an asset. You may find yourself needing to lead change in an environment that is indifferent or even fundamentally hostile to the new. How can you achieve breakthrough change more effectively and efficiently in such an atmosphere?

Stacking the Deck distills the techniques and processes I have learned through direct experience and hindsight into nine logical and sequential steps, described in Part One. These chapters provide practical strategies and real-life stories that illustrate the actions leaders must take when implementing breakthrough change. In reading about the ways top leaders across the business world have navigated change, you can learn from their experiences before you are faced with challenges of your own. Understanding and using these steps will enable you to derive the full benefit of many decades of experience in change leadership—my own and that of other leaders—without needing to spend years acquiring that experience yourself.

As you use the Stacking the Deck process and revisit its steps for each change you tackle, you will find yourself capable of leading breakthrough change faster and more effectively than ever before.

1

Step One: Establishing the Need to Change and a Sense of Urgency

Change has always been part of the DNA of business, but the accelerated pace of technological innovation means that leaders have less time than ever to show a success, recover from a downturn, or make a change stick. There is no fallow period anymore, no time for business as usual, and no patience. If you do not innovate, adapt, and persevere, you will be swallowed up by the hundreds—or thousands—of other people who do what you do and spend all their waking hours thinking of ways to do it better. You have to be nimble and look ahead. Being able to anticipate massive change, like embedding technology to improve your product or service, coming up with a new way to distribute your product, or dealing with a new service's sudden popularity, means that you spend less time knocked on your back, trying to catch your breath.

But no matter how well leaders understand the need for change, the challenges they must face in leading breakthrough change will be enormous. We can't deny that change is part of life. Yet in life and in business, some people embrace change and others actively avoid it. While "change" is theoretically a neutral word, in reality change represents the unknown, and people—some of whom you must lead—almost always find the unknown scary. As Terry Pearce, author of *Leading Out Loud: A Guide for Engaging Others in Creating the Future*, has said, "People hate change. People love progress. The difference is purpose." These words offer an excellent starting point for any discussion about change. Progress implies an improvement, a move forward. And nothing progresses by staying the same.

LINK THE PURPOSE AND MISSION

In leading breakthrough change, we must first convince others—those to whom we report and those on our team—that our proposed change has a positive, necessary, and urgent purpose. To be convincing and to draw people to your leadership team, you have to be clear about the problem or opportunity you are tackling. First with the team and later with the larger organization, you've got to help people believe that the change facing them is actually progress. You will be most successful when you tie the change to the company's mission and show how the change will help achieve it.

If you are rolling your eyes at this reference to the importance of the company's mission, you are not alone. Even though nearly every company has a mission statement that is communicated to all employees from virtually the day they enter the company, and perhaps even in the recruiting process, company mission statements often become a joke among employees. Mission statements simply aren't lived up to in many companies. In these cases, tying the proposed change to a mission that no one believes the company leaders really care about is doomed from the start.

It is beyond the scope of this book to delineate the importance of establishing a strong company culture—the values the company lives by, the actions that make those values real, and a mission that inspires employee passion and commitment. And yet every executive interviewed for this book underscored the critical importance of employees believing in and feeling connected to the corporate culture. When employees believe in a mission, they get excited and passionate about contributing to the company's goals. Thus, connecting a breakthrough change to the company mission and explaining how it contributes to the mission can help employees see and appreciate why a change may be necessary—even critical—to the company's future success.

With more than 25 years as a senior leader in the pharmaceutical and medical device industries, Ginger Graham has a successful track history with change. Now the president and CEO of Two Trees Consulting, she made it clear that many of her largest opportunities and successes have been born of very difficult circumstances. Ginger well understands that "crisis opens the door for change and new solutions." As an example, she explained that at age 37 she became CEO of a privately held business that was in turmoil after a number of leadership changes and product recalls. The company, Advanced Cardiovascular Systems, had leading technology in the world of interventional cardiology. But when Ginger came on board, they were losing market share and had received a warning letter from the FDA. There was finger-pointing and blaming; in those stressful times, she "quickly learned about people and how they operate." Employees, people who were there for the mission, were disillusioned and worried about what would happen next. She was faced with a classic burning platform, a situation in which the need for change is obvious and immediate.

"One of the things that we set about doing was describing our purpose, reminding people of the incredible value of the business. We were literally saving people's lives." This was no exaggeration. "The great need, in our case, was the fact that our products were lifesaving and life-changing and there was a reason that the company had made such a difference and could continue to make a difference.

"We employed this knowledge to reenergize people by engaging them on the purpose of the business. And we did things like bring patients back to all company meetings to really underscore why what we were doing mattered." Putting real faces on heart patients who would have died without the product was an extraordinarily powerful way to underscore the importance of the company's product line and bring the focus back on the company's mission.

Renée James, president of Intel, also emphasized the importance of the connection between the change and the mission: "I think a lot of the big transformational changes are about being on a mission and believing in it. People choose every day to get up and go to work on the mission. At the end of the day, how that mission resonates with your people makes a huge difference. If you ask my tech security team what they do, they would answer, 'We make the world a safer place.' Wouldn't you like to get up every day believing you are making the world a safer place?" If Renée's staff is convinced that a breakthrough change will add to their ability to make the world a safer place, then she is more likely to gain their support for the change.

KNOW THE NEED

Not all of us can logically link the change we're proposing to a need as compelling as saving lives or making the world a safer place. And even if it's only that the absence of change will ultimately lead to a negative outcome, you can find ways to enlist people in the change. In explaining the need and its urgency, you must convince people that staying put is not an acceptable option and will eventually lead to failure.

One problem with staying where you are may be an erosion of competitive position. You may perceive this to be occurring or to be close on the horizon, but others may not yet have noticed. Blackberry and Nokia once had overwhelming advantages in the mobile phone space, but those advantages soon eroded away to nothing. Another reason for change that's even more challenging to communicate is the potential loss of a compelling opportunity to grow. Huge, obvious problems that are clearly threatening are far easier to communicate. For example, the rising strength of the Internet, Amazon, and iTunes left established companies such as Borders, Blockbuster Video, and Tower Records behind. But it's hard to convince people about what isn't obvious to them or already reflected in the hard numbers.

And what if the need seems to be insurmountable or the numbers seem to point to an impossible task? That was certainly the case when Larry Baer and Peter Magowan gathered forces to keep the Giants from being moved from Candlestick Park in San Francisco to Tampa, Florida. When the newly formed ownership group first bought the team in 1993, they took on debt payments of $20 million a year. As Larry, now the Giants' CEO, said, "That was a lot more debt than other clubs and it put us at a competitive disadvantage." Plus, the goal was to build a new park, despite the fact that attempts to build a new park had failed on four recent ballot measures. That part of their vision demanded patience. But the debt wouldn't wait—and the costs of planning and building a park would make that initial debt seem like small change. They needed to attract backers and significantly more funding. And win or lose, new ballpark or not, they had ongoing costs for payroll. When they most needed money and proponents, they were faced with a constant stream of naysayers, from "people in the community all the way through the institution of major league baseball."

Books and case studies are devoted to describing how they did it; Larry conveyed a sense of their driving urgency: "We didn't have time and we didn't know enough to do a business plan. Sure, we could have come up with some fantasy, but we didn't really know what we were getting into. Instead, we had this life or death urgency. We were in crusade mode and assembled smart people who, in the heat of something that they were passionate about, would figure it out. No matter how many brick walls they ran into, people kept trying and they figured it out."

Larry explained the need to just *keep at it* during times like these: "The message we got from the research came down to this: 'Shut up and play ball.' So from soon after acquiring the team in January of 1993 to December of 1995, just shy of three years, we went underground." They worked at it and they paid close attention. When the Sunday paper did a weekend series with suggestions from fans, they took note, knowing that in time, they would implement those suggestions and celebrate the people who came up with the ideas.

Whatever the purpose of the change you are proposing, convincing others of its need requires effort; and it's almost always much more effort than you expect. Even if the need seems logical and inescapable to you, others won't necessarily recognize that at first. People's inability to assess the facts and admit to the need to do something difficult and uncomfortable can seem exasperating. But remember that you've been facing the issues and planning the change for some time; you have to make the case in a compelling and thoughtful way. Even when you do, not everyone will be on board. And while you don't need all the employees on your side, you do certainly need some. For that, you must find the strength to move forward and win over the ones that you can. Getting into their shoes will help.

UNDERSTAND THE BIG PICTURE—AND ALL PERSPECTIVES

When it comes to convincing others, understanding your audience's perspective is paramount. When I took over the branch network at Schwab and began instituting what I thought were small changes, it didn't occur to me that I would need to make a special effort to get the men and women in the branch offices on board. It was clear to *me* that my changes were urgently needed; but it took a long while for me to realize that it sure wasn't clear to the average branch employee. Our perspectives were very different, in part because I had access to information that branch employees did not.

I noticed early in my tenure at Schwab that our corporate culture was wary of sales—almost anti-sales, in fact. Having come from Citibank and Shearson, where selling was perfected to an art form, I found this quite a shift in gears. Schwab ran advertisements with the tagline "No salesman will ever call" to differentiate itself from traditional brokerage houses whose fundamental business model started with cold-calling potential customers. We used a direct-response advertising model to attract new business: the company ran ads and waited for customers to respond. The culture permeated our branches, making our field organization fundamentally reactive rather than proactive.

One can be proactive without being pushy and grow without becoming "sales-y." The question became how to accomplish that change—how to make that progress into a reality—without undermining our customer-centric culture. That required a better understanding of the company's culture.

For the first fifteen years of the company's history, all calls from customers were routed into local branch offices. This setup seems logical at first, but a closer look reveals significant inefficiencies that lead to frequent breakdowns in customer service. During a rush hour (around noon, for example, when customers were on their lunch breaks and had time to call their brokers), some branches would be swamped. Our people were overwhelmed and even missing calls during these high-traffic periods. Meanwhile, employees in another branch office in a different time zone were sitting around doing crossword puzzles, waiting for their phones to ring.

When I asked a branch manager how many new accounts her branch opened weekly, she claimed that the number was about 100. My face must have registered surprise: that seemed like an incredible number for a sales force that never placed outbound calls. She explained that the advertising which Schwab ran was doing well and was actually bringing in people off the street to open new accounts. Clearly we had products that people wanted and our marketing succeeded in engaging people. Customers had demonstrated that they would buy from us if only they knew what we had to offer.

Our first idea was to use the "down" time, when the phones weren't busy, to make outbound calls, rather than have our staff sitting around unproductively. We could thank customers for opening new accounts with us and welcome them to the company. We could even invite them into the branch where we could give them more in-depth information about the services we offered. Schwab wasn't Citibank or Shearson and we didn't want to force it to be that way, but there had to be some kind of happy medium between a selling machine and Schwab's purely reactive strategy.

At the heart of the issue was the fact that our engine of growth— direct-response advertising—was growing less effective as more discount competitors copied our model. If we didn't find another arrow in our growth quiver soon, our success would start to slide. The leadership team understood that this was a serious and urgent issue.

When I introduced these initiatives for proactively contacting customers to Chuck Schwab and Larry Stupski, I thought it would take perhaps two or three years to get this new system substantially in place. The ideas seemed so easy to implement and really not that complex. Making some outbound calls in addition to answering the phone seemed like a natural expansion of our staff's existing job description. Our executive committee was very supportive of this "small change." The problem was that I hadn't really looked at *any* of this from the branch staff's perspective. As a result, I hadn't considered how to help them see the need and urgency for this change.

The difference between selling and what I was proposing seemed clear to me. I wasn't asking people to call customers and urge them to buy shares in a company we were pushing. Instead, it just seemed logical—at least to me—for us to contact our new customers to let them know what our business was and what we had available for them. As far as I was concerned, it wasn't hard-core selling to simply point out that we had IRA accounts or that our customers should start thinking about retirement funds. This is basic customer service. Our customers should know that we didn't offer just stocks but mutual funds and bonds as well. That's a good business decision, good for our customers and good for us.

The more engaged customer outreach would be aimed at getting customers to better understand what Schwab did and the benefits of opening additional accounts and depositing more money with us. If we could get customers to add a custodial account for their children or an IRA, or any other variety of account, we could build our pool of assets. I could see much bigger assets for clients and employees ahead. But first, I needed to better understand the employees I was attempting to lead.

Anticipating Fear and Its Impact

I thought the branch employees would jump at the chance to take on a more challenging, more interesting job that would eventually offer a better rate of pay. From where I was sitting, simply answering phones amounted to little more than clerical work. We were offering them a chance to forge relationships with customers and take on more responsibility. But I initially failed to realize that people liked their jobs as they were.

As far as the branch employees were concerned, we weren't just adding some duties to their job descriptions. We were *fundamentally changing* what they did to something that they expressly did not want to do. Many employees interpreted our proposed changes as a step toward becoming salespeople. For them, our grand plan wasn't an upgrade at all. It was a nightmare!

They didn't realize that change was coming for them either way. Schwab was hardly the only discount brokerage firm around, and all of them were using something pretty close to our model. Just like us, they had people all over the country in little branch offices sitting and waiting for people to call. We needed to do more to set ourselves apart from all the competition—and we had to do it quickly if we wanted to succeed.

One mistake was allowing the situation to be framed as a contrast between doing things as they'd always been done versus changing to something unproven and unappealing. Another was not helping the employees see all the benefits of the alternative. In retrospect, this situation would have been a perfect candidate for the kind of pilot implementation discussed in Chapter Nine—but I hadn't learned that yet. Not surprisingly, we didn't make much progress in transforming the entire branch network, especially with the limited resources then available.

Perhaps the most critical mistake was failing to understand the importance of presenting this change as absolutely necessary and urgent. I did neither, and as a result we struggled. I worked hard at selling this vision of the future, but my efforts did nothing to overcome employees' fear or their reluctance to support this change. The less we progressed, the harder I sold, but since I hadn't fully acknowledged and addressed the fear and inertia that had hold of many employees, I may as well have been speaking a different language.

Understanding and Untangling Fear Responses

Hindsight makes it clear: I should have recognized and understood the employees' fear. It seemed natural to me that people would want what I thought of as a "better" job. I didn't see that many employees had settled into their work and were fearful of having that disrupted. These people knew how to answer phones, how to react, and how to do everything we'd ever asked of them. They were comfortable in their roles. They didn't know if they could make outbound calls or create relationships with customers, and they worried that their jobs would be in jeopardy if they couldn't. These people had spent years building up experience—and value for themselves as employees—and here I was, about to sweep in and take it all away. Changing their job descriptions meant potentially busting everyone back down to the same level of expertise.

That kind of fear is powerful and visceral; it's a purely emotional response. And many leaders go wrong in attempting to counter an emotional response with data or statistics. In *The Charisma Myth*, author Olivia Fox Cabane discusses how psychology is interwoven with business principles. She explains that challenging a person's identity—as I was doing by altering Schwab's branch network—is so fundamentally threatening that sometimes the person completely and involuntarily stops listening. They aren't ignoring you but simply having a physiological fear response that is effectively causing the brain to disengage with what you're saying.

People who are afraid do not behave logically, and they don't respond to logical appeals. Why is it that drowning people have accidentally taken their would-be rescuers down with them? Most often it's because they're so terrified that they're unable to listen to directions and behave in ways that will help, not hinder, their rescue.

Debby Hopkins is CEO of Citi Ventures and chief innovation officer at Citi. She acknowledged that understanding people's perspectives and fears is critical, yet frequently overlooked, in the communication planning process. As she put it, in driving change, some leaders tend toward "an attitude of thinking: 'Wow, we just need to go fix that. That's obvious. That's going to make this great for everybody! Let's go, run, jump!' And that approach may be successful. But it could be a very short-lived success if they haven't attempted to look at it from someone else's perspective. Instead, recognize that the change you're proposing may be low on employees' list of priorities. You have to think, 'Is there a different way I could present this, a different viewpoint that would make this more urgent for employees?' Without that, you could look very cavalier about big decisions and create a backlash you've got to avoid."

Whether a change is simply low on employees' priorities or so dramatic as to require significant effort, how can we smooth the way? What can we do to win over people who are in the throes of powerful emotions? First of all, repetition is important. It's not enough just to announce a change and call it a day. You must give your employees the information again and again and use a variety of methods. Tell them in person, tell them in writing, and tell them via e-mail. Tell them one-on-one and tell them in big groups. It's very likely that not everyone will have heard you correctly the first time. Breakthrough change cannot be accomplished with a single meeting or e-mail blast. Prepare yourself for this reality and know that the remainder of the book, particularly Chapter Three and the leadership communication chapter (Chapter Eleven) will provide more guidance.

UNDERSCORE THE URGENCY

Before you decide to convince anyone else about the change you are proposing, you have to satisfy yourself that change is not just necessary; it's necessary sooner rather than later. You must be willing and able to inspire your team. You have to invest in the change and commit to it with your time, your energy, and your budget. It is not enough to think that the numbers look good: you must truly believe in the purpose behind the change. Be sure that you've considered these issues and that you've honestly pondered and answered the following questions:

- Have I evaluated the numbers for different scenarios? Do they look good?
- Do I truly believe in the purpose behind the change?
- Am I fully convinced of the urgency of the change itself?
- Can I demonstrate that this change is worthwhile and imperative?
- Do we really have to do it *right now*?
- What will occur if we postpone it?

If you have come to a carefully considered conclusion that a breakthrough change is urgently needed, then you will need to drive this forward with all the energy and conviction you can muster. The steps outlined in these chapters will help you along the way, as will the knowledge that driving change is bound to be difficult.

PREPARE FOR RESISTANCE AND CONFLICTS

It is easy to assume that resistance occurs primarily with the frontline employees—but that's not necessarily the case. If what you're proposing is big and bold and strategic, chances are that you will encounter people at all levels of the organization who think it may be easier to do it later. These people may voice their objections by saying, "Let's think about this some more" or "Let's be patient." You might also hear, "Shouldn't we get some more data?" And even, "Are we moving toward the bleeding edge?" All of these may well be valid points, but they may also be a more comfortable way of expressing the feeling that "I'm sorry, but I just don't have it in me to risk that much or work that hard." Overcoming resistance and maintaining momentum require constant effort.

In pondering the question "Do it now or later?" I recalled an experience from my early days at Schwab. At the time, Internet trading was just emerging as a new way to invest, and we had devised a strategy to have two divisions offer online trading: the Charles Schwab online/offline ("offline" meaning phone-based) hybrid service, with a higher price point, and the bare-bones, online-only service that we branded as e.Schwab. We had seen a lot of success with this dual model: the top two online brokers were Charles Schwab and e.Schwab. By almost any metric, our business model was a huge success.

But our customers were growing dissatisfied. They wanted the lower pricing of e.Schwab with the greater service of Charles Schwab. I was getting dozens and then hundreds of letters a month from customers saying they were fed up with being forced to have multiple accounts at different prices. Our disgruntled customers wanted to know why we were making managing their money so inconvenient for them. The plain fact was we were doing it to protect our bottom line. The tiered pricing system of online brokerage was absolutely not customer-oriented; it was all about our own profitability. That was a fundamental violation of Schwab's corporate culture, which encouraged us to always do the right thing for the customer. Furthermore, it was unsustainable.

Although we were receiving hundreds of angry letters, we had millions of customers, so it was not a huge onslaught. If only relative numbers mattered, it would have been easy to look the other way. But it was clear that the rise of low-cost online stock trading firms would lead more customers to either complain or leave us altogether. Behind every letter there were undoubtedly dozens of other customers who were voting with their feet.

I brought this situation to the 10 top executives within the company and posed the central question: Can this state of affairs continue? Did they think that this structure was sustainable? It's not an unheard-of structure; consider the Camry and the Lexus. Both of these cars come from the Toyota Corporation but as two separate brands with two separate price ranges offering fundamentally similar vehicles with different extras, amenities, and brand position. They've thrived for a long time this way, with no apparent backlash from the consumer. The difference between what we were doing at Schwab and the Camry/Lexus strategy was stark, however. We were essentially charging two different fees for the *same core service*, while Toyota had created the brand position of a new car company that sold better cars for more money. Did the comparison to Toyota hold water?

There were strong arguments on either side. After much debate, everyone agreed we needed to change; but how urgently? Some of my colleagues were in favor of making the change sooner rather than later. We were only going to lose more customers the longer we waited. We were the leader in online trading at that time, but our lead would evaporate if we kept the same model in place. And not long after that, we would be struggling to differentiate ourselves from our legions of competitors.

Other colleagues saw it differently. They were concerned that making any kind of big pricing change would lead to a huge dip in our overall market value and potentially affect the public's confidence in our company. They believed the prudent course would be to wait and see how things played out.

Coming together and reaching agreement on how best to proceed became a task for the leadership team. A critical part of the entire change process, it is discussed more thoroughly in Chapter Three. After analyzing the projections, the team knew that Schwab's profitability would take a big hit the year after we implemented this change. Shareholders and Wall Street analysts often see a pricing change (especially one that would drive profitability down by hundreds of millions of dollars) as an early warning sign of business model weakness and they immediately sell stock, driving the stock market value down still more. Ultimately, we decided to go forward and lower our pricing. This was truly a "bet the company" change. If it hadn't worked, the company would have taken a huge hit, possibly an unrecoverable one. As would at least some of us on the leadership team. This was a scary time for everyone—especially the leadership team.

Leaders are bound to face risky changes and resistance. When I recently spoke with John Donahoe, CEO of eBay, he recalled his struggles in convincing an entrenched leadership to make big changes: "When I joined eBay, I thought, 'Oh, my God, we need to change.' I was only partially able to push that idea. The fact that the company had white-hot success in its history worked against it, because even the most capable, confident, accomplished leaders were always hoping that the past was going to come back. I realized that it is human nature to secretly wish for 'the good old days.' And no one wanted to acknowledge that the narrative of success was no longer true. In fact, the more we came under stress, the more there was a tendency to revert back to behaviors and approaches that had worked before."

The responses Donahoe was receiving sounded familiar, as did his next words: "The kind of change we really needed was going to puncture a huge hole in that kind of thinking. We needed to admit that something was wrong and that the past was not coming back. By the time I became CEO in 2008, I had no choice but to confront reality and publically declare that we needed a full-blown turnaround. It felt very risky, but I had to go all-out in terms of bold change."

The need to innovate is a constant, no matter what the business. When I spoke with Starbucks chairman and chief executive officer

Howard Schultz about the challenges the coffee giant encounters in its drive to innovate despite their already enormous success, he said, "Innovation is not a line extension. Innovation has to be disruptive. And we have to teach and imprint curiosity in our company to see around corners."

Schultz mentioned that Starbucks had some innovations in the works. He continued: "The challenge is making sure the mentality of hubris does not set in when you get to this level of success. Can we be as hungry today as we were in 2008 when we had a galvanizing effort because we were in crisis? I think that is the role of the leaders of the company, to maintain that level of ambition and determination while you're winning. But it's really hard."

———

You will often face situations in which you could put off a change but procrastinating would sacrifice certain important benefits. You could always kick the can down the road and make this someone else's problem. But the sooner you take the initiative, the bigger the rewards often are. If you are catching wind of a new opportunity before any of your competitors, it may take them years to respond and catch up. True, it will be easier for them to make their own breakthrough changes after you have already forged a new path. But the lead and the momentum you will have achieved may make catching up to you a daunting proposition. Time and money are two of the three great variables in any business venture, and it will cost your competitors both if they want to advance to your new level.

The third and most important variable? People.

As I saw in the situation at Schwab, a huge amount of resistance can come from your inner circle, the leadership team you rely on for day-to-day success. You must win them over or change their minds—but they must not be allowed to play for time or just pay lip service to the need to change. Bold initiatives require a strong and dedicated team, a team that can work together to develop, strengthen, and maintain momentum. Chapter Two provides guidance on assembling and building that team.

STEP ONE ACTION ITEMS
ESTABLISHING THE NEED TO CHANGE AND A SENSE OF URGENCY

1. What is your company's mission statement? Do employees believe the company is committed to this mission?
2. What is your perspective on the problem you need to solve or the opportunity you need to capture?
3. What evidence do you have of this problem or opportunity?
4. How is this problem or opportunity connected to the company's purpose and mission?
5. Define your stakeholders (customers, employees, leadership, shareholders, vendors).
6. What are your key stakeholders' perspectives on the current state of the business? (Finding real examples for each category of stakeholder can be very helpful.)
7. What customer or employee stories have you heard that articulate these perspectives?
8. Why does the company need to make this change?
9. Why is it important to make this change *now* rather than later? What exactly would be the impact of a delay in moving forward?
10. Are your competitors making similar changes? What are they?
11. What are the potential repercussions—both positive and negative—if you do not make this change?
12. Prepare a concise statement describing the change that needs to happen and why it is urgent.
13. Discuss this statement with your inner circle and test its resonance with them. Does it inspire action? If not, how can you improve the statement?
14. Begin thinking about sharing the statement with a much broader audience and gauging what their reactions may be. (But don't actually begin sharing it until completing Step Three.)

2

Step Two: Assembling and Unifying Your Leadership Team

If you are proposing a large-scale change in your organization, you are undoubtedly passionate about how necessary it is and about crafting a breakthrough vision for the future. But it will be an uphill battle, often more difficult and prone to failure than you may anticipate. No matter how compelling the need and how strong your passion for making the change, achieving and sustaining breakthrough change will require much more than just your passion. No great change has ever been accomplished by one leader alone: one person's skill, charisma, and sheer energy are simply not enough. Leaders must rely on a well-balanced leadership team. Some have the luxury (and responsibility) of hand-selecting this team. Some leaders are brought in to work with an existing group that may or may not already function as a team. Whether you've recruited your own team, inherited one, or face some combination of both, it's your job to actively develop and unify a group that will guide the organization in making your change a reality. This chapter will show you how to do just that.

Stacking the Deck is focused on leading change from within existing organizations that already have histories and processes in place. But whether in the start-up world or in established organizations, the people who most successfully initiate change are the ones who are inspired and fulfilled by being part of something new, challenging, and important. The team that got us to the moon didn't get a billion dollar bonus, even if they might have deserved it. They didn't undertake the project because they expected a big bonus. They devoted themselves to it because it sparked their imaginations and made them feel a part of something much larger and greater than themselves.

Breakthrough change requires that you define the future by imagining a full range of possibilities. It extends beyond making incremental changes in the current reality and often well beyond the comfort zone. Your leadership team must include people who are convinced that the change is both economically and strategically important, despite the barriers and challenges you'll face in undertaking it.

Asking people to come on board is asking them to sign on for something that by its very nature is going to be hard. A big change will always require more resources than you will have available. It will take an enormous amount of time and energy, which have to be mustered against long odds and over a long period. You are looking for pioneers, for people who are comfortable with a greater degree of risk than the average person.

FIND AND NURTURE THE PIONEERS

You must be able to inspire passion in the members of your team and feel confident that they are in turn capable of kindling that spark and dedication in others. Everyone has to be on board. As Starbucks chief executive officer Howard Schultz shared, "You can't achieve bold change if there are people within the organization who doubt its intent and don't feel as if they're part of the idea or the solution, the tactic, and ultimately the decision." You simply can't lead bold change by yourself. Instead, Howard emphasized, you need "a level of consensus and a wide swath of people who believe in the idea and are willing to go to the mat or take the hill. Getting people to believe and having them be 'all in' is key."

When you are creating your leadership team and looking for people to help you make this change happen, consider four key elements:

- Skill
- Experience
- Enthusiasm
- Team fit

Naturally, you want to select people with specialized skill sets and experience in the kind of project you're undertaking. Attitude, as reflected in character, enthusiasm, and team fit, is critical when it comes to change. But the surprising truth is that enthusiasm and team fit may be the most challenging elements to locate.

You need people who are willing to enter unmapped terrain. These pioneers will guide your larger team, usher your change into reality, and serve as ambassadors to the rest of the organization.

Having many of your core group of excited believers come from current staff, embedded as they are within the corporate culture, can be extraordinarily helpful. Your believers are the ideological "early adopters" who can form an all-important bridge between management and the people on the ground who may be skeptical of the change you are driving.

Be sure to dedicate enough of your time and energy to forming the team. You may feel rushed to get the change moving and be tempted to gloss over team formation. But countless transformations have stalled out or even collapsed because very smart, highly motivated, enormously dedicated people thought that they could translate anything they attempted into success. We all want to believe that if we're smart enough and work hard enough, we can do anything we put our minds to. In my experience, and the experience of all the people I've interviewed and known, this is almost never true. Attitude *is* critical, but it's not sufficient. Leaders must find people with the *relevant* experience, and very often—particularly with breakthrough change—that means going outside to recruit the key talent that's needed.

Bringing Outside Experience In

Adding one or two new people from outside the organization can strengthen the team. The experiences—whether successes, failures, or both—that new people bring to the mix can benefit the group and facilitate the change. Bringing in new talent, especially a new executive, is not without risks of its own. Cultural adaptation can be a delicate and perilous process, and you will need to be cognizant of potential interpersonal issues as well as the attitude of any new hires.

Years ago I recruited an enormously talented person for a high-level function, so high that his role made him part of the leadership team. I knew that he had produced brilliant work in the past, and that proved true with us. There was no denying that he was enormously successful at producing breakthrough ideas and concepts. But his bad attitude outweighed the skills he brought to the company. He treated our vendors and our employees with disrespect. He was completely insufferable. No one liked him—and with good cause.

At first I thought I could solve the problem with counseling. I sat him down and explained how his behavior was alienating people, wasn't appropriate for the workplace, and undermined our mission. Over and over, I gave him instruction and advice, but none of it ever seemed to stick.

With the clarity of an outsider, my wife was always telling me that I should just let him go. "That guy is a jerk!" she said. "Just by keeping him around, you are undermining your values. And everyone is watching you." I couldn't deny that she was right. In hiring him, I had assumed a set of shared values. Incorrectly, as it turned out. In keeping him on, I had compromised my values—and Schwab's. In retrospect, I definitely let him get away with his negative behavior for far too long. Eventually, I did the right thing and let him go.

About a year later, I got a call from a senior executive at a Fortune 500 company. "Dave," he said, "I hired a guy a few months ago who used to work for you at Schwab."

"So I understand," I responded. "How's he doing?"

"Well, he's doing great work, but . . ." And I knew exactly what I was going to hear next. He was doing great work, but everyone hated working with him. He was making enemies every time he turned around, and he was eroding team morale. "How do you manage that?" the new boss asked.

"You can't," I said. "Here's my prediction: you will try very hard to get him to change, and he won't. You'll tolerate it until the heat in the organization becomes so great that you realize your own credibility is being threatened. People will start to wonder why you don't just fire him. And then, you will. Just like I did. And you will regret having waited so long."

Needless to say, my colleague on the other end of the phone didn't find this answer very comforting. I had spent months trying to coach a talented but difficult executive into being the team member I needed him to be; but the fact was, he was a solo operator who poisoned everyone around him and who saw no need to change. To no one's surprise, he was fired from his new job a few months later.

Every leader encounters this kind of challenging situation at one point or another. In an ideal world, you would have the time to get a clear sense of character before hiring someone. Unfortunately, the skills we need don't always come perfectly packaged with a great personality, good character, and a team-first mentality. When a huge, challenging initiative is staring you in the face, the temptation may be to recruit someone with hard-to-find skills while overlooking what may be questionable character traits. It's only natural: when you find a candidate with the skills you desperately need, you don't want to find any reason not to hire that person. If the new hire then gets off to a shaky start with the team, it's easy to chalk it up to adjustment jitters rather than face the fact that you may have made a hiring mistake. However, it is always better to identify these problems early and deal with them before they fester, since without intervention the problem will only get worse.

A toxic person who does great work may make you look good for a while. But bear in mind that even with counseling and training, when people are under pressure they often default to old, negative habits. Let this go on too long and your own leadership will soon be called into question: what kind of leader sacrifices the unity and cohesion of the team? Do corporate values matter or don't they? In the end, unless the person genuinely acknowledges the need to change and is willing to put in the considerable effort required, keeping these types of people around is usually not worth the cost to the team and to the organization. Making compromises on character to get the skills you need rarely works out. Be sure to get a clear sense of character before hiring someone. And if you make a mistake, deal with it quickly.

Reconfiguring the Team, as Needed

Of course, there is a difference between someone who is never going to be a team player and someone who is simply on the wrong team. Let's say you introduce a new person into a group of people who have all been working together for 10 years. You can expect that the team will be a bit disrupted initially and that some clashes of personality will arise either with or because of the new member. Sometimes, however, like trading athletes to a different team, when you move people into a different group the fresh start allows them to blossom. It's reasonable to try a new situation for someone who is not working out, as long as the person's fundamental attitude, level of commitment, and work product merit the benefit of the doubt.

Then there are the famously challenging people who will either take most of a project on their own shoulders or build a specialized team around them that can tolerate—or even thrive under—a demanding, potentially hostile boss. More often than not these people do not succeed because they require such a unique hothouse atmosphere to do their work. Like much of our role as leaders, managing difficult personalities is a delicate balance.

TAKE STEPS TO UNIFY THE TEAM

Even with the right people, you have to unify the team and manage your people in the right way. True teamwork—real, effective cooperation and communication between team members—is rare and it's a huge edge that you will need when embarking on a breakthrough change initiative. More than the plans you develop or the financial resources at your disposal, it's your *people* and the way you lead them that will make the difference.

How you behave as a leader and as a team player is both critical and too easily overlooked (but not by the team). Although most people describe themselves as team players, this often means, "I love teams, as long as they follow all of my suggestions." Much as I hate to admit it, that quote could have been from me in the earlier stages of my career, when I functioned largely on my own and then as the head of teams in a management capacity. But the shift from being a solo manager leading a team to being a manager of a larger operation is minor when compared to the monumental shift of managing an operation *and* being part of an executive team. That next level—when you're working on an executive team with colleagues—can present an entirely different set of challenges and require a new set of skills.

Fortunately, having recognized that our team needed help, our boss brought in a leadership coach to work with the entire team. I soon realized just how desperately I was in need of remedial help. It's not easy to change and it certainly wasn't easy to let go of my desire to control all the elements of any major initiative. My executive coaches, including Terry Pearce, encouraged me to confront this weakness, and I've worked hard at improving. Those experiences all underlie the importance of making a constant effort to surround yourself with talent and working at improving yourself and others in the process.

One way to gauge your own ability is to ask your team to give you the answers to the following questions, on a periodic basis:

1. What do I do particularly well that I should do more of and build on?
2. What do I do poorly that is hurting the team and needs my attention and commitment to change?
3. How could I do better? What actions would help me improve and improve our team performance?
4. What do I spend my time on that I need to do more of?
5. What do I spend time and energy on that I need to do less of, delegate to someone else, or stop altogether?
6. How else could I improve my performance and that of our team?

Your team needs to know that you'll treat their answers as constructive and strictly anonymous. With that understanding, they may deliver up some surprising answers. Be sure to have a session with the team in which you review the feedback and let them know what you plan to do to respond to their suggestions. You have asked for help and your credibility will rest on the humility, candor, and follow-through you demonstrate in your response.

If reading your team's input is difficult for you, take particular care in preparing yourself for this meeting. The team will be waiting to see how you handle their feedback. The more difficult the feedback, the more important that you demonstrate a genuine desire to improve and gratitude for the team members' honesty. How you initiate the conversation, how you express yourself, how you frame any follow-up questions of your own or from the team, even how you carry yourself: every detail speaks volumes. If you have a leadership coach or other outside resource, talk through the meeting in advance, in detail. Understand that this follow-up meeting is an opportunity to improve yourself, recognize and model the value of candor, and build trust. The grace with which you handle this conversation is crucial for you and for the team.

If continuous personal improvement is one of your goals, try to keep current in works on business management and leadership—and to read the ones with lasting value. For anyone who is or aspires to be a leader, I recommend Patrick Lencioni's best-selling book, *The Five Dysfunctions of a Team: A Leadership Fable*. Lencioni describes major dysfunctions that may threaten to destroy any team; he presents these dysfunctions as a sort of cascade. Number one, absence of trust, fuels number two, fear of conflict; fear of conflict then fuels lack of commitment. Eventually you cascade further into avoidance of accountability and finally inattention to results, and your team and its mission are in shambles. This progression has been reflected time and again in my personal experience and in that of hundreds of executives I have taught over the years. Encountering any of these dysfunctions is not necessarily a red flag that you've selected the wrong people or screwed something up along the way. It may simply be a natural part of learning to trust, which is absolutely foundational.

Building Trust

Absence of trust is the source of a lot of team dysfunction, and establishing trust must start when a team is first formed. In fact, this is how you begin to build a high-functioning team.

The first time I went to an executive offsite where we were asked to talk about ourselves, our life story, our passions, our hopes, and dreams, I thought to myself, "I can't believe we are wasting time on this nonsense. Let's discuss what we need to work on to drive our growing success!" I didn't think my impatience was unusual; I expected that most hard-driving executives also viewed this kind of stuff as a giant waste of time. But I was wrong. As it turned out, many of my presumptions about other people were off the mark, sometimes even by 180 degrees.

Getting people together and encouraging them to talk about themselves can in fact be a great trust builder—when done well. The leader's job hinges on enabling people to understand each other, to understand their motivations and their character. Your team members reveal themselves when they speak. They explain where they're coming from and discuss the experiences that have shaped them. Trust and cooperation can grow. On the flip side, some people use sharing opportunities to tell self-aggrandizing stories that actually foster resentment. It's important to shape and drive these situations to make sure that the stories actually bring people together rather than create walls between them. Since not every executive has the skills to lead such a discussion, investing in an experienced facilitator can be very worthwhile.

Team members need to get to know each other. Spending time in an offsite setting allows people to discover the experiences that have shaped others' skills and perspectives, and to understand others' personal values. Even though an offsite may at times appear as a mere respite from the office, the time spent building the team, working on team dynamics, and learning why a specific initiative is worthy of the team's time and energy is far from some boondoggle. The trust we need for driving change will come when we understand each other's motivations, the why behind what we do. Without that insight, people can too often ascribe words and actions to the wrong motivation and thus resist change. Spending time together enables that understanding and rapport to develop. Lencioni's book offers some suggestions on team building, as do other books in the market. Team-building efforts are an important investment and part of the process of building trust.

Facing Conflict

It is not easy to face conflicts without first establishing trust. Trust is more than a feeling of security or an absence of fear. Trust enables assured reliance on the character, ability, strength, motivation, and truthfulness of others. If you do not establish trust—both between yourself and your team and among individual team members—a fear of conflict will dominate team members' interactions. Recognize that trust and fear are especially closely linked and that fear stunts meaningful dialogue. To have real discussions that get at real concerns, team members have to be willing to confront one another and resolve any conflicts. Your job is to create an environment where people feel safe doing so without fearing personal reprisals or punishment. People need time together and shared experiences for trust to grow, for getting comfortable with others' motivations, character, and intent. If you don't create that safe environment, you'll wind up with a team full of people going out of their way to avoid conflicts, people who are more interested in not rocking the boat than in fully exploring potential problems.

There's no one right way to create a safe environment for dialogue; each corporate culture is different. In some places you may find a very lively, almost combative culture of debate; in others, politeness is highly valued. Of course, there are larger cultural differences to think of as well. The issues of fear and conflict and how to deal with them are fundamentally different in an American corporation versus a Chinese corporation, for example. As with all the issues ahead of you, you have to devise a solution that fits the context. Once you have established a foundation of trust and constructive conflict, resistance decreases and processes move more smoothly.

Focusing the Leadership Team

You cannot achieve team unity overnight. We don't have one meeting or one team-building retreat and then pledge our undying commitment to one another and to the change initiative. But we can begin the process, and urge people toward a place where they understand debate and discussion not as personal attack but as a vital part of working through issues and refining the change. In doing so, we will also combine our efforts into focusing on commitment, accountability, and results to ensure the long-range success of the change.

These are topics that are front of mind for many leaders. Among the challenges that Debby Hopkins faces at Citi is finding ways to get one of the world's largest banks to innovate—both around the world and ahead of smaller, more nimble competitors. As she said, "When I think of experiences that I had 10 years ago versus now, the impact of disruption driven by technology, regulatory changes, and globalization creates a far more complicated landscape to traverse."

Our conversation turned to deepening our understanding of how people work, individually and as part of a team. We were aiming at the same target, just using slightly different tools.

Understanding Work Styles Debby told her leadership team that she wanted to do something to bring the team together and help them function more effectively, and to think about how each member works individually. As she said, "One option was the classic Myers-Briggs assessment. But I suspect it's an outdated tool." She learned of a comparatively new system that the company's recruiters had just been starting to use and were finding very powerful. "It's called the Style of Influence—and exactly what we do is try to influence things," she said. "It's an incredibly impactful exercise that takes very little time to complete. In fact, you can go online and do it in about 10 or 12 minutes."

To hear Debby explain it, the new tool was, over and over again, nailing people's preferred style of operating, so much so that the entire team engaged in this powerful exercise. Our increased understanding of all of the types of people on the team can overcome what may seem to be insurmountable odds en route to success. These efforts together give us a better chance at being successful in finding a path to the future.

Understanding Team Dynamics Debby is certainly not alone in her search for ways to unify and improve her team. Team dynamics can make all the difference. The number of systems and organizations focused on team dynamics is some indicator that getting those dynamics right is not necessarily a smooth journey. The notion that a team gets better simply by working together is not necessarily true. Practice alone simply can't get you there unless you're practicing the right skills and at the appropriate level. Practicing the wrong skills with the wrong dynamics can lead straight to a dead end.

Team leaders are wise to drive continuous improvement of their teams by measuring and assessing their team dynamics. Changing behavior is difficult, and without compelling, actionable feedback it is virtually impossible.

A variety of systems are available to help focus leaders on areas of interpersonal dynamics that have the biggest impact on business performance and output. Often team members provide feedback on the team leader and rate their team on carefully defined attributes of a high-performing team. The results can help the leader and the team members recognize areas for improvement and set goals for improving. I recently employed a tool called Team Insights™ that measures levels of collaboration, engagement, morale, and trust and allows teams to focus their efforts on areas of weakness. This book's website provides links to some of the tools that might help leaders understand and improve the workings of their teams.

—————

You need to assemble, build, and strengthen the leadership team, always making it clear what the team has been convened to do. One function it is not charged with is making final decisions. A team exists to perfect the change, but even the best of teams require you to take point on the major decisions. A mentor's simple phrase still rings in my head: "A voice is not a vote." A voice is an opportunity to raise objections and make suggestions. It is not a vote, and a leadership team is not a democracy.

This is where the idea of commitment comes in. You need to stand behind each decision you make and consistently carry out the plan you've all developed. The commitment starts at the top with you and then spreads out through the rest of the team.

You do have the final say, and that should be clear to your team members. But the more these individuals contribute to a plan, the more personally invested they become. And this is where account-ability comes in. If a team develops a plan for change and commits to carrying it out, then all members ideally have a stake in it. Cultivating a sense of ownership in the debate process can increase each person's sense of responsibility for resultant decisions. And in the long term, that will encourage everyone's attention to the results.

With your leadership team now assembled and unified, you are ready for the hard work ahead. You've established the need and urgency for change in Chapter One and have begun assembling and unifying the leadership team in Chapter Two. You now need to craft your compelling vision of the future. That's the subject of Chapter Three.

STEP TWO ACTION ITEMS
ASSEMBLING AND UNIFYING YOUR LEADERSHIP TEAM

1. What skill set do you personally need in order to make the change successful? Do you have these skills? What's your strategy for dealing with your own skill deficiencies?
2. What skills, experiences, and backgrounds do you want members of the leadership team to have?
3. What character traits do you want members of your team to possess (for example, analytical, energetic, task master)?
4a. If you are *inheriting* a team:
    i. How did their previous manager lead and motivate the team? How does this differ from your style?
    ii. How do these people stack up with respect to items 2 and 3 above?
    iii. How will you complement their deficiencies: new hires? internal recruiting? promotions? training? consultants?
4b. If you have the flexibility to *recruit* your own team, develop a list of candidates who align with the attributes in items 2 and 3 above.
    i. What can you point to as evidence of each person's level of enthusiasm for the initiative? of each person's ability to lead the aspect of the change they would be responsible for?
    ii. What value proposition will you describe to get them on board?
    iii. Now you can begin to recruit. Listen carefully to the responses, positive and negative, that potential team members provide as you recruit. Their suggestions and concerns can help you fine-tune your thinking.
    iv. Once you have selected a team, you need to galvanize it. Start focusing on the need to change and on the dynamics of the team.
5. What is the team's purpose and vision? What are you convening these people to do? (This will be important to come back to throughout the breakthrough change program.) Review your thinking on the need to change, from Step One.

6. Conduct an offsite kickoff meeting with the team, in which you walk through the mission, expectations, and Lencioni's Five Dysfunctions. Make sure people understand each of the dysfunctions and how to mitigate them. The focus is on getting to know one another, setting expectations, and building trust. Through your discussions, you'll develop a strategy for building teamwork and trust as an ongoing activity.

7. What training or opportunities can you offer to team members to strengthen their value to the team and help them support the change you are advocating?

8. Find ways to periodically gather data on the team's perspectives of their own performance, so that the team can improve over time.

9. Gather anonymous feedback from the team on *your* performance so that you can improve. Discuss the feedback with the team and concentrate on your ability to effectively hear and take action on the constructive criticism from the team. Be aware: this is not easy.

3

Step Three: Developing and Communicating a Clear and Compelling Vision of the Future

Once you have your leadership team in place, you and your team need to be ready to envision and communicate the future in such a vivid and irresistible way that everyone around you understands your vision and shares your passion for it. At this point, you've already seen and become convinced of the need for breakthrough change. But convincing others can be much more difficult and time consuming than you might first anticipate. Leading change has often been compared to preparing for and leading an expedition, and with good reason. You need to be sure that everyone can work together and that they all have the same goal in sight.

And "everyone" is not just the leadership team, but everyone around you. You won't accomplish this step in a conversation or two. You are going to have to deliver a carefully crafted message to every group of stakeholders, a message with a central core as well as add-ons that can be adapted for each unique audience. Your technology team will require a different emphasis from that of operations, which will be different still from that of frontline sales, marketing, human resources, and every other group of stakeholders. Perhaps you'll spend one morning explaining to one group of people how your vision of the future will increase profits, and the same afternoon telling another group how the proposed change will kick start operational efficiency or improve customer service. Each time you explain your vision is an important message to others and a useful process for you. By emphasizing different parts of your vision to different people, you can develop a more precise, more holistic picture of your proposed changes. All of your messages become part of your vision for a better, more successful future.

These concepts may seem very similar to those of Step One, establishing a need to change, and in some ways they are. Both of these steps are fundamentally about creating or revealing dissatisfaction with the way things are today. However, in the earlier step, we were simply attempting to convince others that *the status quo is unacceptable* and the way we are doing things today no longer works; we need to do something different as we move into the future. In Step Three, we develop and present a very *specific idea* of what that "something different" is. In most cases, this means comparing the present to a future that is very different. The challenges are to inspire people—many of whom have been comfortable where they are—and to get them excited and involved enough that they want to head into that future, that they become eager to participate in this expedition to the new.

Up until this point in the Stacking the Deck process, only a few people in the organization have heard your presentation on the need for urgent change. They're the ones with the authority to approve your initiative and those you've recruited to help you craft a vision for the future. After all, you can't go around the company telling layers of management and employees that prospects are dreadful, horrible threats loom, and change is urgently needed—but you don't yet have a clue as to what that change is, let alone how to implement it. To do so would create all kinds of chaos. Instead, you've talked about the need for change with a relatively small circle, many of whom will partner with you and own the task of crafting a breakthrough vision of the future and the plan to get there.

HEADING INTO THE BLUE

Sometimes breakthrough change does not involve fixing or adapting an existing organization, but creating something entirely new and fresh. To do so, we must be willing to create a future out of nothing, much as airline JetBlue did in 1999. Mike and Dave Barger are two of

JetBlue's founding team members. Mike is the former head of JetBlue Flight Operations and his brother, Dave, is the current CEO.

This low-cost airline emerged from a particularly vivid imagining of the future, fueled by dissatisfaction with the airline services that were then available. At the time, most airlines were not focused on the customer experience and cared little for employee morale. The JetBlue founders—mostly executives from other airlines—were drawn together by one central question: "What's wrong with airlines today?" A lot, as it turned out.

By clearly laying out what they didn't like about current airline operations, the leaders at JetBlue knew they could more accurately identify their own goals. Early on, the major players got together in New York City to focus on three questions:

1. Is it possible to build an airline that people actually like?
2. Is it possible to build a company that people like to work *for*?
3. Is it possible to build a low-cost airline in a high-cost marketplace?

On the first day, they brainstormed and wrote down everything they disliked about the airline industry on a huge sheet of butcher paper. These included issues with customer relations, the treatment of employees and general operations, and anything else they found lacking. The homework for that first night was to take those problems and try to solve them.

The leaders soon discovered that they could solve nearly every one of these problems with what they began to call "the radical application of common sense." Several individuals mentioned how frustrating it is for customers when they're waiting at the gate and the departure time comes and goes without anyone providing any information. The JetBlue founders decided that it would be their corporate policy to simply tell passengers what was happening when a plane missed its departure time. Today this seems like an obvious solution, but it wasn't common practice in the industry at the time.

In the process of going through the list they had developed, the team broke down their "radical common sense" solutions to a series of ideas: safety, care, integrity, fun, and passion. These words represented a response to the dreary landscape of air travel as it existed and formed an ideological framework and a set of corporate values for the new company. Over the course of those days, the JetBlue team moved from the realization that the flaws in the existing airline business ran very deep to a vivid picture of a future airline that resolved those issues.

In this case, leadership wasn't faced with the challenge of making changes in an existing company; they were starting something entirely new. In time, the dramatic shifts they proposed and sought would affect the airline industry as a whole. Building the JetBlue future was a collaborative effort from the beginning. Any resistance or pushback the new airline would face would come primarily from the market, not from disgruntled employees or previously dissatisfied customers. Furthermore, the JetBlue leadership team came together out of a genuine desire to be part of something great. They did not need to be urged to upset the status quo; they had already chosen to be active agents of change.

LEAVING THE STATUS QUO AND CREATING THE FUTURE

You need not be part of a start-up to rethink your industry and create a compelling vision of the future. The brainstorming technique that JetBlue used, often called "blue-sky thinking," can be used successfully in practically any business setting. You may encounter resistance if your stakeholders are already deeply invested in maintaining the status quo; but the mind-set of change can ultimately become unstoppable in any situation.

Whether you are starting anew or bringing change to an existing organization, you must give people a clear—and strongly compelling—vision of the future: where the organization is going and their role in the new future.

Momentum is critical in the early steps of breakthrough change. To begin building that momentum, you first need to start communicating the vision to everyone in your company. You must make your commitment to the vision of the future—the breakthrough change you are driving—real to your people and do everything possible to get everyone in the same state of mind. But no matter what your energy level may be, you can't do this alone. You must first get the entire leadership team fully on board so that they too are actively creating this future.

Clarifying the Vision

When Schwab undertook the pricing change for the Internet discussed in Chapter One, the need for change wasn't obvious and immediate to everyone in the company. We didn't have a clear "burning platform" to urge people to adopt the change. We were enormously profitable at the time, and the proposed change would require us to take a big financial hit, at least in the short term.

How then to create a sense of urgency around this change and unite people, when we could have put it off until later? Yes, we had done the projections and knew that without the pricing change, our lead in the marketplace would soon evaporate. But numbers don't necessarily persuade and excite people. We needed something more, namely, to conjure two different visions of the future. To convince the team that Schwab's position wasn't as secure as some might think, I reached out to four of the disgruntled customers who had written me letters detailing their frustrations with the tiered Internet pricing system then in place. I asked them to meet with our leadership team and tell them about the grievances they'd cited.

With each of these high-revenue customers right in front of them, describing in detail how they felt the company was doing them a disservice and eroding their trust in the process, the problem became hard to ignore. These long-standing, high-caliber customers felt that the company was not meeting their needs and instead violating the customer compact. If we couldn't adjust, they were ready to take their business elsewhere. Conveying this information directly to the team was a critical part of establishing an urgent need to change. Our customers' testimonials demonstrated to the leadership team that this unappealing version of our future had already begun to take root. Their stories, delivered in person and with great passion, were far more persuasive than any tidy columns of numbers on a spreadsheet might have been.

We began to realize that acting quickly and decisively could halt this tide of customer dissatisfaction and reestablish ourselves as the responsive, customer-first company we had always been. Even if we did experience a temporary revenue or profit slump with this change (which would eliminate approximately 25 percent of Schwab's level of profitability at the time), our market share leadership of trades and accounts would actually skyrocket.

Since the Internet brokerage ecosystem was growing rapidly and becoming intensely more competitive every day, we knew that we needed to act. Just as we had predicted, the stock value went down promptly after we made the change, plummeting nearly 50 percent in days. We had anticipated this and were even prepared to weather a few years of poor stock performance. We had been honest with our board, analysts, and investors about this aspect of the change, never glossing over the risks. Everyone knew the change was going to seriously lower our profits for a time.

And then, also as we had predicted, the customers stopped trickling away. They began trading more and more often. By quickly adapting to fulfill customer desires, we had distinguished ourselves, reinforced our customer-first reputation, and positioned ourselves for a huge wave of volume growth eventually followed by a wave of revenue and profit growth as well. Prospective new customers began to show interest in the new pricing scheme. We recovered faster than even our most hopeful projections had suggested. Our stock climbed back to its pre-change value—and then doubled in worth by the end of the year. That same year, our stock valuation passed that of Merrill Lynch. In twelve months, we had gone from a crazy company tossing away our lead in the market to a bunch of geniuses who had done an end run around disaster.

Strengthening the Leadership Team with Constructive Debate

Facing the facts and debating the alternatives turned out to be an extremely healthy team-building activity for our leadership. At the beginning, not everyone was convinced this change was necessary. But as we dug into our customer metrics and explored our trends, and analyzed financial projections of how the change process would unfold, the team gelled around the need and we all came to own the vision for where we were going: one Charles Schwab with a highly competitive pricing structure for our online trades. Our depth of understanding and our combined passion about the need for the change enabled us to sell the need for a pricing change to the next layer of leadership, to the hundreds of managers who ran all parts of the company, and ultimately to all 11,500 employees. It was very clear to all of us—those who carried the message and those who heard it—that this change was urgent, necessary, and connected to the mission of our company, and would lead to an exciting future for Charles Schwab.

SHOWING YOUR PASSION

Whether it's creating a better airline or a new pricing structure, you have to believe in the change passionately—and share that passion over the long haul. Intel's Renée James feels strongly that transformational change hinges on belief in a mission: "In technology, you have to invent the future. You have to imagine what could be—and then what has to happen in order for that to be true."

Renée describes the role of personal character and personal passion in making change a reality: "People judge the reality of a vision and the possibility of its truth by the passion of the leader. The words you choose are important and your actions, on a daily basis, even more so." People won't follow leaders who *say* all the right things but don't act according to what they claim they believe. They want to see their leaders making personal commitments and taking personal risks. Leaders have to be willing to publicly stake their reputations on the ideas they are advocating.

Passion is something that you can't teach and that you have to keep in full supply. As Renée explains, "You spend all your time operating in the change state, which requires a lot of energy and a lot of repetition. You must always put your conversations into the strategic context. You've got to keep it up until the job is done." No matter how many times you've said it or in how many venues, you have to be consistent—"to help people see concretely what they could only understand abstractly before." Then, "once they see it, once the lightbulb goes off, they've got it. They understand; they say, 'We can do this!'"

That lightbulb moment is part of what keeps Renée going. But for Larry Baer, whose vision of a new stadium and a top-ranked team in San Francisco, which was "not a baseball town," explaining the vision wasn't enough. Instead of talking nonstop, the leadership team effectively went dark while they developed their plan and their vision. Then, when it was time to build support, they found a very tangible way to test their concept and share the vision.

As Larry told me, "Probably the best $50,000 we ever spent was to build a model of our new ballpark. We took it to the commuter train stations and lobbies of downtown high rises and office buildings and showed it to people. And people bought into that vision. We even built a full-scale model of a luxury box to get reactions. And it was clear people were buying into our vision."

Buy into it they did. Baer and his leadership team had displayed and promoted the model at the right moment; the model drew positive attention and transformed into reality as the team took new shape. When the new ballpark opened to sellout crowds in 2000, it quickly became a record-setting ballpark, against the odds.

———

There were two recurring themes in all of the interviews I conducted for this book:

1. The critical need to communicate a compelling vision of the future
2. The critical need to communicate that message over and over

Leaders need to spread the message to different groups and at multiple times to the same group, in different ways and in various situations. The ability to lead change rests on the leader's character and skills as a communicator. Developing yourself in these areas is an immersive process, as deep as it is rewarding. It is vital to each of the Stacking the Deck steps and transcends all of them. Developing your communication skills should be at the top of your list.

In this chapter, we have discussed *what* you need to communicate to the organization. Chapter Eleven spends more time on the *how* of that communication effort. This is likely to be just the beginning of your development in this arena.

In a sense, communicating the vision behind the breakthrough change effort is never over; it's something you must repeat and constantly reinforce. To do this well requires passion, patience, and understanding. You will need to develop and practice your communication skills and your listening skills, all along the way. A healthy dose of curiosity is invaluable, both to be open to the new and to continue learning at every opportunity. With curiosity, you may see that any opposition or resistance you encounter can also reveal the problems you'll have to solve. Recognizing the issues early gives you a huge advantage. What to do when you spot them is the subject of Chapter Four.

STEP THREE ACTION ITEMS
DEVELOPING AND COMMUNICATING A CLEAR
AND COMPELLING VISION OF THE FUTURE

Developing a Compelling Vision of the Future

1. Go back and review your completed action items for Step One. What has changed in your thinking since then? How have you refined your perspective?

2. Work with your new leadership team to brainstorm alternative strategies for solving problems or seizing opportunities. How will you get people's support?

3. Who are the key stakeholders (individuals and groups) you need to get on board immediately?

4. Which key stakeholders are most likely to be advocates of this change and help communicate the vision?

5. In the action items for Step One, you reviewed the perspectives of key stakeholders (customers, employees, leadership, shareholders, vendors). How can you personalize the vision to reflect these perspectives?

6. What benefits will the change have on key stakeholders? How does the proposed change tie to the mission of the company?

7. Revisiting your answer to item 11 in Step One, if you do not make a change, what are the repercussions, both positive and negative? Does your team agree with this? If not, how and why? What therefore has to change?

(continued)

(continued)

Communicating the Compelling Vision of the Future

Before you delve into the details of these action items, read Chapter Eleven and go through the Framework for Personal Leadership Communication Guide© to frame your message and consider how you will connect it to your personal experiences and the stories that will bring it to life.

1. Identify who will be most affected by the change and which of your leaders, including yourself, would be best at carrying the change message to the organization. Do not underestimate the importance of this role; it can be almost a full-time job. This is best accomplished when more than one leader is carrying the message, although consistency can be challenging.
2. Craft a draft message that ties the change to the mission and values of the company. Use your inner circle as a sounding board to help you craft and refine your message. Use outside consultants if possible.
3. What part of the message is core and must be consistent to all audiences? Which part or parts can be tailored?
4. How will your audience members' roles change with the new vision? How will the changes impact them? Make it personal, acknowledge that you understand how their jobs/behaviors/rewards will change and what that may look or feel like.
5. List all existing communication vehicles that can be leveraged (weekly e-mails from CEO, homepage of internal website, TVs in common areas, and so on).
6. How often will you communicate results or progress to your internal and external stakeholders?
7. Develop a holistic communication plan, detailing all communications, frequency, content owners, approvals, and more.
8. Identify all opportunities for face-to-face communications. Begin with planning and conducting face-to-face meetings as your foundation. Ask and answer questions and learn as much as possible about what people are concerned about.
9. Look for small venues to begin communications programs. Start with smaller groups to test the message.
10. Prepare a list of potential questions and craft answers.

11. Who else can you employ to help communicate your message: customers? former customers? retired and revered former leaders? frontline employees? others?

12. Plan and conduct a more high-profile kickoff event for the breakthrough change. (Consider broadcasting it to the entire organization.)

13. Are road shows needed in order to communicate the launch of the breakthrough change in a face-to-face way to internal and external stakeholders? Who should do the road shows, and for which audiences? Establish content, timing, and so on.

14. Create a mechanism for people to ask questions and raise concerns on an ongoing basis.

15. Think about the questions and concerns that come in as learning opportunities. Take those questions and concerns that seem most universal and design ways to craft and communicate the answers to a broader audience.

16. After building the foundation with personal, face-to-face communications, begin to leverage electronic communications (e-mails, homepage, and others).

17. Remain personally visible throughout the effort. Talk with employees in the cafeteria, walk the floors, and so on.

18. Focus on any and all opportunities to build positive momentum and the perception that progress is being made.

19. Continue meeting with smaller groups to hear their concerns. Don't just rely on reports that bubble up. Hear it and see it for yourself.

20. Prepare a plan to communicate the basic message over and over. Embrace the notion that your people need to hear this message many times; each time, their takeaway is likely to evolve, even if your message remains essentially unchanged.

4

Step Four: Planning Ahead for Known and Unknown Barriers

Every project comes with a host of potential barriers to success. Part of developing a solid plan for implementation involves thinking through these roadblocks before you encounter them.

The fourth step in the Stacking the Deck process is all about anticipating problems as you are planning, and confronting these problems before they derail your efforts. You might well wonder if this isn't simply a piece of the planning process (Step Five). The answer is not a simple yes or no; it's more involved.

The planning process will require a team of highly engaged people, a team that may begin to extend beyond the inner team we talked about in Step Two. It will also require time to develop the fully built-out design for a bold, breakthrough change. However, your initiative can be undermined and derailed before it has even left the station if you haven't considered and dealt with the most obvious and potentially difficult barriers at the earliest stages of the project.

Ideally you will think through potential problems as an extension of your original vision. Breakthrough change typically originates when we observe trends and realize that something has to be done differently. We have to extend the reach of that critical thinking to consider the possible effects of the change we are proposing. Unfortunately, you cannot anticipate all problems. In general, however, the early or initial difficulties you will encounter when introducing breakthrough change fall into four broad categories. So many great change initiatives are given up for lost or destroyed because of these difficulties that I refer to them as the "Bermuda Quadrangle"—a tongue-in-cheek reference to the Bermuda Triangle, the area in the western part of the North Atlantic roughly between Florida, Bermuda, and Puerto Rico known for unexplained disappearances of ships, planes, and people.

MAPPING THE BERMUDA QUADRANGLE

We have already discussed some of the emotional, social, and psychological issues that leaders need to address in all steps of the change process. So it should come as no surprise that people issues underlie all points of the Bermuda Quadrangle. Just as some of the dangers in the Bermuda Triangle stem from the shallow shoals that lie beneath the surface, the issues that compose the Bermuda Quadrangle—resistance, skills, processes, and company culture—are not always clearly marked or identified. But they exist, to varying degrees. Further, the danger represented by each point of the quadrangle can shift, becoming stronger and more significant without warning. You need to be aware and on the lookout for these issues as you plan and then execute the changes you propose.

People Resist Change

What will people resist? What will they embrace? What can you do to allay their fears about the change? The brevity of these questions is deceiving. They are difficult questions that must be addressed early and with an open mind. As one who is drawn to change, I've learned (with many reminders) how important it is to recognize that change looks different depending on where one stands. What seems like a promising path to the future from one perspective can look like an overwhelmingly dangerous leap from another. It's the leader's job to prepare people for the journey ahead. That's no small task, and to get it right demands the empathy and patience to see others' concerns and points of view.

Steve Ellis, CEO of Asurion, a technology protection service company, shared with me his theory about resistance to change and about people problems: "You'll deal with three different groups of people and they are not evenly distributed. Often, we have 5 percent who are going to embrace the change and 15 percent who never will. Then we've got 80 percent who are in the middle, who can make the change, but need some help to do so.

"The people who are going to embrace change are the ones you've got to put in the leadership roles to drive the process." As Steve said, the best breakthrough change processes he has seen "have very quickly gotten that group of the 5 percent focused on creating the Proof of Concept pilot. In time, the way is led by—and infused with—that 5 percent's energy, vision, and passion."

As for those "who are going to resist change no matter what, you have to identify them quickly." Steve acknowledges how challenging this can be: "All too often, companies take way too long to face this reality because those in leadership positions want to make room for long-tenured staff in the future of the company. Often, the more tenured people just can't make the changes you need them to make and will have to be replaced. This is the difficult job the organization is counting on you to do."

But there is a payoff to this hard work: "If you ignite and empower the 5 percent while eliminating the drag of the 15 percent, you can move the 80 percent with astonishing speed."

We both understood just how important it is to get everyone on board. Without that 80 percent working with you, you simply can't get a realistic assessment of what it's going to take to get the change propagated across the organization—and you certainly can't get there with any speed.

Skills Are Missing

You have to be sure you have the people you need in order to implement the changes—and that they have (or can readily acquire) the new skills and new perspective the change demands. Recognize that a great attitude is required but is not sufficient. Part of your advance planning, therefore, must be a careful assessment of what skills will be needed, how they can be developed in-house, and where you can find them outside. A few thoughts to consider:

- What array of skills will this project demand?

- Do we currently have people with the specific, targeted skills and experiences that we need to successfully complete this project?
- Do we have enough people with these skills and experiences to implement the changes?
- If the answer to either of the two previous questions is no, how much time do we have before we need to be fully staffed?
- Will the organization tolerate the time required to train current employees or recruit new people?
- If the necessary skills don't currently exist in the organization, how soon can we find people with the necessary skills and experience to bring believability to the idea that the project can succeed?
- How and where can we find the necessary support people?
- If the company has previously hired for a totally different skill set, what other strategies can we use?

You'll have to find ways to get people to adapt, or else actively recruit new people. Most likely you'll do both. The most difficult piece of this equation is making a realistic assessment of whether the people you have either possess or can learn the skills you need in order to get where you need to go. If the answer is no—and it often is—then you'll likely have the wrenching task of cutting staff who have been with you for a long while to make room for the new people.

As you'll see in later chapters, one of the more unfortunate realities of leading breakthrough change is that not everyone can follow you.

Processes Are Rigid

Next is the problem of overly rigid processes and procedures. If you are proposing a change to established processes and procedures, you may be up against years of institutional habits and mind-sets. You'll need to determine where the company is set in its ways and decide what it will take to change those procedures and mind-sets. Don't underestimate the challenge this presents. You must make sure that those above you, either your boss or maybe the board, understand and support the change you are proposing.

Bear in mind that organizations are built and structured for reliability, consistency, predictability, and control. A company's processes and procedures have been designed to deliver these results. Many employees' self-image and perception of their personal worth are rooted in their knowledge of these processes and reinforced by their own heartfelt belief in the processes' critical importance to the company.

But breakthrough change isn't reliable, consistent, or predictable. The new control procedures put in place to deal with the new reality may be immature and not yet up to the task. And that is only the beginning. The changes themselves will often challenge the fundamental necessity or even the relevance of these long-trusted and tenured processes, which are typically rather inflexible. In our new age of high technology, mobile connectedness, and global competition, every long-standing process will undergo scrutiny and will change to some degree. Examples include how you deliver customer service, measure advertising, develop and test technology, schedule and administer meetings, design employee benefits, and measure morale.

Company Culture Is Unyielding

The decision that your boss or board makes is heavily influenced by the final category of risk marking the Bermuda Quadrangle: corporate culture. You need to think about the breakthrough changes you're proposing in the context of the entire enterprise. Does this change fit in with the values of the existing corporate culture? If it does, how can you best make that connection clear?

In the decision to add what I referred to as "customer relationship development" to the branch employee job description at Schwab, I was seen as violating the corporate cultural value that "sales was not in the cultural DNA of Schwab." People often asked me, "Does Chuck know you are pushing this idea?" As a result, this change was an incredible uphill battle and took much longer than it should have.

In contrast, an equally bold initiative involved moving some of our inbound calls from the branches to a call center. This was a huge investment for us at the time and was very disruptive to our employees. But since we framed and "sold" it as a major improvement in our ability to handle peak-period call volumes, employees perceived it as congruent with our cultural value of "improved customer service" and they readily accepted the change.

Sometimes the difference lies in the questions you ask. Consider the difference between asking, "Does the initiative fit or not fit our culture and our values?" versus framing the question as, "Can we find a way to connect this initiative to our culture and values such that it is a new expression of those values rather than something that's in conflict with them?"

If the change is so dramatic that it cannot be made to fit within the existing corporate cultural values, then you must prepare for a long uphill battle. Those employees who are most threatened by the project will use this conflict with values and traditions as a lever to undermine your leadership and drive a stake into the project's legitimate fit in the company. You can overcome this, but doing so will take a lot of effort and will be a huge distraction. Better to find a way to avoid this problem, a way to make the project fit the culture and its values; by avoiding the problem, you can create more momentum for the initiative.

COMPOUNDING THE DANGERS

As if navigating the Bermuda Quadrangle weren't already difficult enough, the problems represented in the four points of the quadrangle are rarely so distinct. Often they can't be compartmentalized into one of these four barriers. For example, a people problem can also be a skill problem as well as a corporate culture problem; a processes problem can also be a culture problem.

The difficulties that eBay's CEO John Donahoe encountered in presenting the urgency of the need for change (described in Chapter One) stemmed in large part from resistance and an entrenched company culture. That combination rendered even smart, capable operators surprisingly ineffective. As a result, John explained, he "ended up replacing eighty of my top hundred people—really, really good people—at eBay in the beginning." John had quickly realized that people's tendencies to compare the changes being made to where the company had been a year ago or two years ago were not constructive. When people inside the company would say, "eBay has gotten 25 percent better," John had to remind them that in the same time frame Amazon had gotten 50 percent better, putting eBay only halfway to where it needed to be. As John explained, eventually he "had to bring in people from the outside that had no history with the company. These were people who walked in and said, 'Oh, we're 50 percent behind!' They were able to grab on to change far more aggressively, with far less personal baggage. It's all about finding the change agents that exist inside the culture. And then identifying people who block change as well. Unfortunately, some of the people that block change are often some of the most talented people."

The resistance and entrenched company culture that John described were akin to the issues we had faced at Schwab in instituting the changes to the branch network. When we began to transition to customer development (sales), we had not yet developed and nurtured the skills that employees would need for the additional calls and interactions with customers that they would be undertaking as part of this change. This skill gap was quickly uncovered as soon as employees were asked to change the way they viewed their roles. Ultimately, over the course of five years, approximately 80 percent of the branch employees were unable to make the transition to our new model of service. This change hurled us through all points of the Bermuda Quadrangle in what felt like slow motion; it was our own perfect storm. We all learned from it—and it underscored the importance of advance planning and anticipating barriers.

PLANNING FOR THE UNEXPECTED

When you are navigating the Bermuda Quadrangle, you need an advance plan, and you also need to stay flexible, accepting that you will come upon barriers and issues unexpectedly. A good plan is all about anticipation. You have to look not just at current issues but at ones that may crop up only after the change goes into effect.

The way to prepare for the unexpected is to explicitly talk it out, and not just inside your head. You can't do it alone. Gather executives, responsible business partners, and any other people whose involvement is critical to the change you propose and ask them all to think seriously about how the change might be received within the organization, outside of the organization, and what could go wrong. In developing the ideas for your breakthrough change, as you think about ways of broadening your reach and expanding your net, be sure to get more perspectives as early as possible to better appreciate what the initial reactions might be.

Once you are excited about the vision and are completely convinced that it's worthy of time, energy, and passion, it can be hard to take a step back to fully appreciate how others might see it from a wholly different point of view. By bringing others into the process of discovery and imagination, together you can be more realistic about how people will view the change and how you can best present the ideas.

Examine Potential Resistance

Leaders must anticipate resistance and even look for specific issues of resistance in advance. Experience has taught me that among the first tasks of the leadership team should be making comprehensive lists of the ways employees are going to push back; determining the time, assets, and staff you'll need to make the plan work; and carefully considering the ways the change will—or might seem to—conflict with the corporate culture as it stands.

Take the time to explore and think about the risks and the uncertainties ahead and do so in detail so that you can eventually manage them proactively and create comprehensive ways to defuse these issues. While it's tempting to lump risks and uncertainties together (and perhaps underestimate both as a consequence), be careful to tease out the differences. Risks are measurable: while you may not be able to predict with certainty exactly what will happen, you can make a reasonable estimate of the odds of success versus the odds of the project going wrong. In contrast, uncertainties are both unknown and unknowable: these appear on the horizon with no warning and require that you adapt and adjust in the moment.

When we were preparing to implement the Internet pricing change at Schwab, we were committed to identifying all the risks and potential issues we possibly could. So we held a meeting with our top two layers of management. We broke the group up into teams of 10 or so and asked them to imagine that they were having a meeting with the next layer of executives. Where did they expect to see pushback and resistance to the projects? What could they identify as roadblocks? What questions might they be asked? What other information might that next layer of executives need?

In addition to having them anticipate that next level of rollout, we were hoping to learn what objections and fears they themselves held, fears they might not fully or frankly voice on their own behalf. To be an effective change leader, you must truly come to the conversation curious, meaning you arrive ready to listen and learn, not just to sell, persuade, and convince. If you are completely wedded to your approach, then you cannot listen and learn with a completely open mind.

Coming to the conversation curious is far removed from just going through the motions. It requires a level of openness and engagement that may be new for some leaders. It can be very hard to hear responses and questions that make you uncomfortable or that seem to undermine the approach you've taken. But those critiques, those questions, and those issues are out there and are part of the workplace. Refusing to acknowledge them doesn't make them disappear; in fact, avoiding them undermines your credibility as a leader.

This process of anticipating people's specific resistance requires you to put yourself in the shoes of others. Problems surprise us because we are coming at situations from our own perspective without taking into account the perspectives that others may have. What might seem a minor shift to you may well be a huge issue that someone else will lose sleep over. Getting your top people together and creating an open forum is a great way to get inside their heads in a nonthreatening atmosphere. Individuals may not have been comfortable raising these kinds of issues one-on-one for fear of being alone in their fears or objections. Ask for theoretical objections. When we did this at Schwab, the objections came quickly:

- Our share price will plummet.
- Call centers will lose calls and become less important.
- Our stock options will be wiped out.
- Our bonuses will be gone.
- Branches will close.
- There will have to be massive layoffs.
- Our fundamental business model and profitability will be threatened. We will permanently lower our profit margin, and therefore the value of our company.

Some objections came in the form of questions:

- Will our image be damaged if we lower prices to compete with upstart online brokers?
- Are we giving credibility to upstart brokers who are operating in lower tiers?
- Will this be seen as admitting that the upstart brokers who were underpricing us were a competitive threat that we needed to respond to?

These concerns, and many others that surfaced at the same time, helped provide a broader and also more in-depth understanding of people's perspectives. All of these were real concerns and once having actually put them on the table, we could begin to resolve them.

Tempting as it may be to skip this step or rush through it en route to the change you're driving, if you miss this opportunity or fail to present it in a way that makes it real and allows for honest feedback, the gap in understanding could have dire consequences for the overall success of your breakthrough change initiative. And even if you do gather and incorporate feedback into the overall plan, consider that there may still be issues that haven't been uncovered. People may simply be too enmeshed in the history or the culture to have the perspective they really need. In some circumstances, you may need an entirely new perspective, from outside.

Outside Experts Can Sharpen the Focus

Using outsiders can help you better anticipate the barriers you will face or even see the opportunities that are already in front of you. From 2000 to 2004, we faced several downsizings at Schwab as our revenues continued to contract in the face of huge stock market headwinds. We conducted these layoffs without outside help and we stumbled because layoffs were a very difficult fit with our culture.

After almost four years of mediocre efforts at downsizing, we finally made the decision to bring in outside consultants. They immediately saw hundreds of millions of dollars of potential cost savings that we had missed. Similarly, when Intel faced the need to downsize from 2005 to 2007, what needed to be done was also a difficult cultural fit. Intel's CEO and CFO ultimately brought in the same outside consultants Schwab had used, and the company managed to save billions. Intel's CFO later credited the success of this effort to the perspective we gained from our consulting team, and these consultants ended up working with us for almost a decade on a broad host of assignments. In a company very entrenched in operating its own way, we learned we could benefit greatly from advisors who had exceptional experiences that were outside of our own. To name a few examples, these included embedding a philosophy of continuous rightsizing of corporate functions, improved processes around acquisition analytics and post-deal assessments, new ways of thinking about capital structure, and the rational deployment of debt.

In my experiences and those of my interviewees, outside consultants play a huge role in the success of breakthrough change. They are valuable repositories of new experiences, new wisdom, and challenging perspectives—including the critical perspective that can debunk corporate mythologies.

Step Four addresses significant issues you may face in developing and implementing plans for a breakthrough change. Keeping the dangers represented in the Bermuda Quadrangle in mind, ask yourself, "What resistance, gaps in skill sets, problems in processes, and cultural issues are likely to arise if we install the new, breakthrough change we decided on in Step Three?"

When you are leading breakthrough change, you'll discover that human nature, market conditions, and inertia have already stacked the deck against you. The best way to restack the deck in your favor is to take the time, in advance, to think through what problems are likely to arise. If you look down the road, you can develop a plan that either prevents those issues from becoming true problems or responds to them so effectively that they won't fester into something worse or gather momentum across the organization. That part of the planning process is the focus of Chapter Five.

STEP FOUR ACTION ITEMS
PLANNING AHEAD FOR KNOWN
AND UNKNOWN BARRIERS

1. There is always resistance to change. Where do you and your leadership team believe it will it come from in this case? Outside stakeholders (customers, vendors, analysts)? Inside stakeholders (finance, HR)? Others?
2. For each group, what is the logical source and emotional source of their resistance?
3. What is the case-by-case plan to deal with this resistance to either neutralize it or turn it completely around?
4. As you and the leadership team dealt with each group to work on their resistance, what did you learn that you didn't know before? What can be useful?
5. Share all the results from items 1–4 with your leadership team. Prepare a plan to use what you have learned to overcome resistance. Work in Steps Six and Seven will also be helpful.
6. What skills that are needed for the initiative are missing or in short supply in the organization today?
7. Start developing a plan to recruit the talent and skills you need (see Step Eight).
8. Outline the existing processes and procedures that could inhibit or slow down the change effort (for example, number and level of approvers needed to approve funding or even the basics of the bonus program that will apply to project team members).
9. What can you do to mitigate the processes that most inhibit the progress?
10. Does the current culture of the organization generally embrace breakthrough change? What evidence do you have for this point of view?
11. Will cultural beliefs about organizational values and or traditional business practices make this specific change more difficult? If so, specifically identify these beliefs.

12. Are there stories or experiences in the organization's history that defy the current perceived values and culture and support the proposed change? How can you employ this in your communications plan to overcome the cultural resistance?

13. Assemble your leadership team and conduct a brainstorming session about what other barriers this change effort is likely to encounter. List those barriers and then develop plans for how to mitigate them.

14. In what ways might you and the team modify the change effort to make it more readily accepted?

5

Step Five: Creating a Workable Plan

The first three steps of *Stacking the Deck* focused on concepts that combine substance and emotion: establishing the need for change, building and focusing the leadership team, moving people to buy into a dynamic vision of the future, and inspiring them even when the going gets tough. All of these require an intellectual understanding of how processes and organizations are structured, the creativity to imagine a better future state, the emotional awareness to appreciate others' perspectives, and the ability to complement your talents and capabilities with those of others. Step Four introduced us to the practical action needed to identify and avoid barriers. As we enter Step Five, we get down to the nitty-gritty of planning the details of breakthrough change.

If you have read through the book and are now working through the Stacking the Deck steps with an actual change initiative, you already have an idea of the impact your change will have. You also have a sense of the problems and barriers you may face as you implement it. Now you need to translate the inspiring vision of the future that you and your team have developed into a workable, real-world plan. Here you must draw heavily on your practical and strategic management experience.

PLANNING AND BUDGETING

Assuming that you know (or have studied) the basics of planning and budgeting, this chapter—and this book in general—takes that understanding one step beyond. Here we discuss how planning and budgeting change when we scale up and initiate breakthrough change.

By definition, bold, breakthrough changes aren't predictable, reliable, or controllable in the classic sense. Yet most organizational systems are focused on safely maintaining all the indicators that organizations like—predictability, reliability, control, and risk minimization—within a certain comfort zone. Breakthrough change initiatives fly in the face of each of those qualities.

Having known each other from our years at Citibank, Dick Kovacevich and I readily jumped into these topics during our conversation about leading change. Dick was the chairman and CEO of Wells Fargo from 1998 to 2007 and was instrumental in leading its growth. He shared some very strong observations regarding the mistakes organizations make when they try to create a plan for breakthrough change. "Companies need to have multiple types of plans. There is a short-term quantitative budget, a short-term action item list, and then a strategic plan. The first two—short-term quantitative budget and short-term action items—are what you prepare and use to run the everyday business and to report out to your various constituencies." Dick emphasized that he doesn't put a breakthrough change in either of those categories. We both well understood that far from minimizing risk, breakthrough change initiatives introduce new risk into the organization.

Dick continued, "The strategic plan, what some may call a three-to-five year plan, is not very quantitative or detailed. What's most important there are the big changes and lofty goals and visions you set for the company rather than hard quantifiable metrics. With the strategic plan, we do have a process for managing the project and figuring out what we are going to do and how much we are going to spend over five years, but it is analyzed totally separate from budgeting."

The traditional corporate management systems for planning, budgeting, performance appraisal, and the like are not made to accommodate breakthrough change and, in fact, work contrary to the goals and needs of such a change. So when you propose a breakthrough change, you will often find yourself needing to dramatically modify and rethink how these basic processes fundamentally work.

Dick went on to say, "The only budgeting aspect of the strategic plan is the cost that we have to put into our budget to fund projects we are working on. But we have to be careful. One of the biggest mistakes people make in change is looking at projects through a quantitative lens (metrics or timeline) when we don't yet have any idea of what we're really talking about." He emphasized the danger inherent in this approach, stating that "we are marching into the unknown with a breakthrough change, and simply cannot have a *detailed* budget since we don't yet know enough to *precisely* estimate and quantify the economics."

By way of illustration, he wound up with a story that is vintage Dick Kovacevich: "When I was CEO of Wells Fargo, we wanted to grow the average number of financial products our customers had with us. Of the 14 products we measured, our average customer had 1.7, and I wanted to grow to 8. The reason I chose 8? It rhymes with GREAT! That's it: put a big hairy goal out there without knowing how you will achieve it. Then, once you've set that reach goal, you have to go build the strategic plan to get there."

At the time of our interview, in August 2013, Dick explained that 31 percent of all their customers then had eight or more products with Wells Fargo. Could be that Dick's attitude and the culture he encouraged are integral to Wells Fargo's current status as the most highly valued banking institution in the world.

MAKING ASSESSMENTS: FROM THE PRESENT TO THE FUTURE

When the founders of JetBlue were first contemplating their new airline, they brainstormed with blue-sky thinking and used a blank piece of paper, sketching out the broad strokes of what they were hoping to accomplish. Starting anew and long-term planning do have certain parallels: the need to assess where you are, where you want to be, and how to get there. These assessments are vital to leading breakthrough change, whether you are starting from scratch, reshaping an aspect of the business, entering a new market, or looking to expand your reach.

Initial Assessment: Where We Are

When Ron Graves became chief executive of Pinkberry in 2007, the frozen yogurt company already had launched more than 20 stores in Los Angeles and New York City. Ron sensed that given "the brand's passionate and cult-like following, Pinkberry had the potential to be a global brand." But instead of quickly rolling out more stores, Graves took a year to assess the organization. As he put it, "I knew we'd be growing fast, so laying a solid foundation with the infrastructure that would support rapid growth was paramount." His process was in three stages:

- He built a team of investors, board members, and management personnel with the capabilities to guide the company through a global expansion.
- Ron and his team then clarified Pinkberry's mission and core values, including entrepreneurial spirit, uncompromising quality, and customer delight—guiding principles so foundational to Pinkberry's success that he personally teaches them to all new employees and franchisees.
- He then outlined a strategy for growth that included franchisees who shared the company's values, had multiunit operating experience, had deep local roots and knowledge, and were financially sound.

Once its foundation was set, Pinkberry hit the domestic and international market in full force. The company expanded into the Middle East in 2009 and opened more than 50 stores in the region. Since then, it has continued its domestic and international expansion and as of 2014 has nearly 250 stores across 27 states and in 19 countries. The early assessment was a major factor in the company's ability to "establish a balance between the structure and discipline necessary to scale without compromising our values." This is a balancing act that

Ron says the company "must fight for every day, then, now, and in the future."

Whatever the business and circumstances, virtually all plans start with a thorough assessment of "where we are" (WWA). This assessment should take into account not just operations and processes, but all other factors that contribute to a company or organization's position in the marketplace. You want to look at factors such as competitive position, customer satisfaction and quality of output, productivity and efficiency, human resource considerations, and more. Any or all of these aspects may need to change in order to get your vision off the ground.

You must also gauge all the skills you are going to need over the course of the initiative: marketing, sales, operational efficiency, familiarity with social networking, and whatever else your specific change initiative requires. Do you have those skills on your team, and if not, where can you get them? Whether it's consulting firms, staffing agencies, or simply going to other departments within the company, you need to have a plan to get the expertise you require (we'll return to this critical subject in Chapter Eight).

There are many junctures where an inexperienced or overconfident leader can make a misstep. In the early planning stage, for example, many managers simply project the current state of affairs into the future, including some marginal improvements in productivity and quality. It's fine to make simple, linear projections if you are planning for incremental change. In fact, doing so is a predictable, reliable, low-risk approach. And often this may be the right course of action. If, however, you are aiming for breakthrough change, you need to do much more.

Assessment for Breakthrough Change: Where We Want to Be

Breakthrough change is not linear. It's not an incremental momentum plan. Instead it demands a leap to a fundamentally new and different position. Assuming we're after breakthrough change, the second big assessment revolves around "where we want to be" (WWWTB). It's your job as the leader of the breakthrough change to fully articulate your concept of the future. Whether from one's education, habits, or from a desire to take the safe course, leaders often have a strong tendency to define WWWTB as a simple projection of WWA (where we are) with perhaps modest or even aggressive improvement. But truly breakthrough change is a chance to substantially redefine the future to be something very new and different, perhaps a competitive leap forward. What will success look like in this new situation? How will we measure that success?

Citi's Debby Hopkins and I discussed the need to expand the conversation from the start, so that we aren't defining the future by what we're doing today. As she put it, "You want to change the dialogue that goes on in determining a future path. When you get people engaged in the conversation of options, thinking about the range of possibilities—the full range of possibilities—they're more able to get away from their linear way of thinking. That's particularly important in this world of the fast-changing business model and constant reinvention."

The conversations you want to encourage—creative, wonderfully energizing discussions—become the starting point in contemplating WWWTB. These are true dialogues, open-ended conversations; they are more than one-way, or even two-way. Be sure that you and your people are imagining the most timely, highest-potential breakthrough. What you don't want is for people to picture just more of the same, only faster. At this stage, you want to think imaginatively, envisioning a different future. Contemplate the galaxy of that future. When it's time to make choices, you will be able to choose from a wide array of possibilities. Even then, as much as WWWTB is a specific goal, we must also recognize that change, particularly breakthrough change, is a process of exploration and discovery along the way. We must leave ourselves the space to learn and the flexibility to redefine our destination—all without our economics completely falling apart.

Later in the process, when you're determining how to bring WWWTB to reality, you'll be more precise as you narrow the neighborhood to an address via strategic planning processes and decision making. For that stage, which we turn to next, Intel's Renée James emphasized the need to be pragmatic about where you really are and where you are going, acknowledging the personal risk and fear that come with "stopping doing something that's made you successful. You may be staking your everything and maybe your company's everything on this leap toward the future."

Assessment for Action: How Do We Get There?

The first two assessments lead logically to the third: "how do we get there?" (HDWGT). That is, how do we get from where we are (WWA) to where we want to be (WWWTB)? The second assessment, WWWTB, is the vision question that we first discussed in Step Three. The difference here is that rather than painting a big, sweeping picture of the future, we must now define that future as a set of specific goals, deliverables, and metrics, because now we are creating the actual plan. When you can fully answer the "how," breaking it down in terms of partitioning, metrics, people, and pilots (Steps Six through Nine), then you will have developed a meaningful plan of action. Where this stage in breakthrough change differs from the usual planning process is an even greater recognition of the unforeseen. Because your pathway to the future is not continuous or predictable, you need to leave room in the plan for missteps, dead ends, delays, and a great deal of learning along the way.

In discussing the challenges of getting a group from where you are to where you want to be, Renée James had this to say: "If you cannot 'bridge,' if you cannot get your people to see from where they are to where they are going, they will never put their trust in you and the project. If you can't tell them the first step—and how that first step translates into a possible future—it's really hard for them to move at all." And that is exactly why you must consider, carefully and thoroughly, each of the questions inherent in the three assessments.

PLANNING COMPONENTS

Like many other business plans, the plan for a breakthrough change has the following key components:

- Goals and deliverables

- Tasks
- Deadlines
- Capital and other resources
- People

You'll often need to deal with these components differently in a plan for breakthrough change.

Goals and Deliverables

The first component, in which you define goals and deliverables, must occur multiple times over the life of the initiative. In contrast to planning an incremental change, you don't know exactly what the outcome will be at the beginning of a breakthrough change initiative. If, however, you are using the Stacking the Deck process, you will have a reasonably good idea. You should have a clear need to change and a compelling vision of the future. But that isn't the same as a specific set of executable goals you can move toward. You can usually partition breakthrough change into a number of discrete initiatives having defined deliverables. By dividing your overall goal into smaller, step-by-step goals, you will have a series of checkpoints that you can use to determine if you are on track. When you subdivide a single, giant goal into smaller targets, you allow for more control and momentum building.

Breaking down the initiative into a series of goals is also a useful way to deal with potential shortages of time and money. If resources and time frames are tight, scaling down the deliverable definition may be a solution. For example, this could involve an initial launch in a limited number of locations rather than a complete rollout. Your new deliverable becomes that first small pilot implementation, and you will reevaluate the overall plan after that portion is completed. (A detailed discussion of pilot implementations is in Chapter Nine.)

Tasks

Once you have the broad strokes of a plan, you must lay out the tasks you need to accomplish. This part of the planning process remains the same for most project and operational plans, whether the change is incremental or breakthrough. Push-back and resistance are nearly inevitable with most changes—and they will cause delays and cost money. You must anticipate and plan for this, to avoid or at least minimize disappointments and difficult conversations with your superiors as you miss deadlines and struggle to hit your budgets.

Deadlines

Deadlines are incredibly important in projects of this nature. You must be constantly reinforcing the importance of critical deadlines as they relate to key deliverables. There are often many moving parts in breakthrough initiatives and they are often interrelated. Pause or remove one and everything grinds to a halt. A single delay along a critical path will push everything back. Delays are the enemy of ambitious initiatives. They eat away at resources, team credibility, and momentum. You combat delay the same way leaders approach other problems: anticipate, anticipate, anticipate. Build an expectation of delays into your plan, and don't cut time frames too close to the bone.

You must build the sense that every key deadline will somehow be met. It may require weekends and late nights, but the team must—and will—rise to the occasion. Without this attitude, practice, and commitment, slippage will pile upon slippage. A few small lapses can seem innocent on their own, but if they build on one another they can derail your whole initiative. You must develop an ambitious (and realistic) plan and guide the team toward the goals. In the process, you need to build and maintain commitment and a spirit of determination. We'll discuss this in greater detail when we go beyond the nine steps of Stacking the Deck and discuss leadership communication, in Chapter Eleven.

Capital and Other Resources

In examining the gap between where we are and where we want to be, leaders will begin to identify the resources necessary to get there. There's likely to be a series of economic and institutional limits on those resources. As a result, the budgets typically awarded for these projects seem much tighter to those who are responsible for the actual outcomes. You need to negotiate from a place of strength and knowledge to secure the best possible framework for your change initiative. It is far wiser to negotiate your needs up front, even before signing on, because you can discuss weaknesses and strengths of the project without having them reflect on you.

Debby Hopkins and I discussed the difficulties of developing a financial plan for breakthrough change, particularly one that takes us into entirely new territory with inherently unknown outcomes. She was clear in her belief that any big change needs "a maverick, a zealot who is passionate about the change—that this is where we need to go—and a phased approach." She explained that Citi uses "a stage-gated process for funding innovation projects." This allows Citi to maintain "our fundamental point of view about the proposed change: this could be huge, this could create a whole new market in financial services that has yet to be defined. We develop hypotheses that we need to start proving." She continued, saying that as they "progress through the gates and closer to market, we then introduce more traditional measures and targets." Using the stage-gated system allows Citi to "explore big ideas without committing big money."

Debby's process of putting limits—putting gates—on funding provides a reality check and time for reevaluation. It makes a great deal of sense. Leaders may allow their enthusiasm for a project's vision to result in underestimating potential difficulties and challenges. It is all too easy to imagine that a project will be less difficult and less expensive than it really will be, that the capital and other resources we've been allotted will be more than enough to complete the project. We do this in part because change often seems "simple," perhaps even obvious, and partly because humans have a penchant for wishful thinking.

While I've learned just how hard change can be, I persist as a change junkie. The question that rings in my head is often "How hard can it be?" Often, too, it is addressing that very question with honesty and depth that's difficult—and critical. This tendency to underestimate applies to time and resource requirements (such as money and personnel). Given the unpredictability of breakthrough change initiatives, budgetary overruns do not necessarily mean the project is failing. Instead, if planning is thorough and information is shared early, problems that might otherwise seem disastrous can be overcome.

John Donahoe shared a story from eBay that underscored the need for assessment and making an honest—brutally honest—plan for the future. "One of my CFO's best moves was a very honest assessment of our financial future. We had our investor meeting right in the dark depths of 2009 when the global economy was in free fall. At the time, no one was even giving quarterly guidance because things were so bad and prospects were so grim. My CFO made me go out and put our financial goals for the next three years on the table. I said, in effect, 'In year one, we're going to lose more share and it's going to get worse. In year two, it will get a little bit better. And here's where we expect to be three years from now.'"

I could picture the reaction he'd faced, and John confirmed it. "The investors and analysts didn't love any of it. They certainly didn't love year one and year two and they didn't even totally love year three. But having put those numbers out there liberated everyone. We told the truth about what was possible and conceivable. It gave us the freedom to get worse before we got better and it gave us a baseline against which we could measure success." John explained that they were able to build a sense of success internally and externally because they outstripped their established goals. Having described the future as his CFO advised and putting "it into an external context turned out to be incredibly important. When we weren't making progress I could say, 'This is what we said we were going to do. And we're on track, or we're going to surpass what we said here.' And even if no external force is giving us credit or recognition, this is how we said we would measure our success. And we can build on that."

John's story demonstrates just how powerful an honest projection, clearly communicated, can be. In the bleak financial atmosphere of the time, the temptation must have been to present a rosier picture, or even simply remain silent as others did. But John's CFO was exactly right: creating a plan for the future may mean acknowledging that the future will be worse before it gets better.

Furthermore, by communicating his vision of the future in this way, John avoided some of the biggest risk factors and bolstered his credibility. By giving conservative time and profitability estimates, he increased the chances that he would not go over his deadlines or miss his financial projections. Plus, when eBay performed better than expected, it was celebrated as an even greater success. That's good planning for uncertainty, in a nutshell: Acknowledge the risks and challenges. Lay out your plan. Don't underestimate the time and resources required, and then rally your troops to deliver.

John's story speaks to being thorough in your projections and helping people see the big picture. Keep remembering that any breakthrough change initiative will be full of uncertainty. To balance that, the initiative must offer significant benefits to the organization. It must provide a compelling return on the capital that is being invested. In other words, don't take on a bold, risky project with a $10 million investment for an estimated return of $12 million or even $15 million. For that level of investment you probably want to go into it expecting a $25–$30 million payback. Then, if you meet unexpected overruns in time and money, there is still a reasonable likelihood that your now $14 million project is still a worthwhile investment. This is why venture capitalists typically won't even look at projects with less than a 30 percent internal rate of return (IRR) and a better-than-four-times multiple on invested capital. They know that most surprises don't improve the economics of returns; instead, they depress them. You need to adopt a similar philosophy. You shouldn't even begin down the path of breakthrough change unless the potential ultimate success has a payback sufficient to justify the time, energy, resources, and risk.

Finally, remember that any breakthrough change is likely to require other resources in addition to capital. Even if these resources exist within the organization (for example, vacant facilities, spare work space, technical support, accounting), they must also be described and included in the budget.

People

People go hand in hand with more physical resources. Often the only way to combat a shortage of funds or labor is with an excess of passion. This goes back to finding your pioneers and getting them on board quickly. You need people who are committed, excited, and willing to put in the extra time and effort. You need to get twelve-hour days for the price of eight, seven-day weeks for the price of five. You need people who appreciate this project for its intrinsic value rather than solely for monetary compensation. Because the unfortunate fact is, success in breakthrough change initiatives doesn't usually produce economic windfalls for the employees involved. It can, however, produce great amounts of psychic income that will keep the team engaged.

The mission and people's connection to it can be enormous assets, whatever the financial budget—of the company or of its people. Along those lines, Renée James is fully aware that many people in her organization have achieved financial success and are far from being driven by a monthly paycheck. Instead what keeps them coming to work is the understanding that their company "can change the world—and that they have the possibility of changing the world every single day." The impetus that the mission provides is powerful and compelling. The depth of the mission is also important, for as Terry Pearce frequently reminded me, "People will give effort for money but they will give their lives for meaning."

PLANNING FOR RISKS AND THE INEVITABLE QUESTIONS

It's true that breakthrough change takes time—and it takes even longer if things go wrong. As explained in Step Four, advance thinking and planning can help you navigate through a number of barriers, but not all. The planning process you undertake in Step Five is perhaps the best time to take a preventative look at risk factors, to analyze and attempt to mitigate them proactively. Risk factors can come from inside and outside the company. Regulatory changes or strategic moves by competitors can also put roadblocks in your path.

These kinds of obstacles are generally harder to anticipate than the internal risks leaders face in bringing the initiative to the world (as described in Chapter Ten).

The sheer number of outside complications that might influence your organization make it virtually impossible to develop enough Plan Bs to counter every vulnerability. But you must constantly be looking—and planning—ahead. You should expect your colleagues to ask you, "What might go wrong, and what will you do about it?" You must be prepared to answer these questions. You can have contingency plans ready for the most likely problems. Certainly many risks you simply can't control, but you have to demonstrate that you've thought about these issues and developed logical reactions.

As much as we try to identify and plan to deal with risk, there will always be uncertainty when we are breaking new ground. We must learn to live with it. Indeed our ability to lead and inspire when the outcome is not at all guaranteed is an important part of this process. Thinking about risks in advance, having contingency plans in place, and learning to expect the unexpected will be enormously helpful when you have to act fast, whether because of changes in the business, the market, or other circumstances.

Rudy Giuliani was mayor of New York during the 9/11 attacks. The city had experienced terrorist attacks in the past, though of course not on the same scale. And in a city the size of New York, so much can go wrong: the subways can stop working; the power grid can fail; hospitals can go dark; storms can create havoc. While the events of 9/11 had been unforeseen, many aspects of the after-effects of the attacks were foreseeable and plans had already been created to mitigate them. So the emergency plan that Giuliani and the city's leadership put together in the minutes and hours following the attack effectively consisted of stitching together various emergency plans for other contingencies—plans that had already been created and thought through. Thus the unthinkable results of 9/11 became somewhat manageable, because crisis plans on a smaller scale already existed.

Certainly, when compared to what Giuliani, his team, and all of New York faced in the aftermath of 9/11, leading breakthrough change seems considerably easier and less fraught. Yet advance planning is key, whatever the goal and whatever the future. We need to conduct assessments and create plans that will help get us from where we are to where we want to be, and be flexible enough to adapt along the way. We should also plan for a category of "unknown unknowns," just as the engineers at NASA have for decades.

The most detailed of plans may need modification. And sometimes, as we'll see in the next chapter, a plan improves by being partitioned into smaller, more readily managed pieces in order to increase the likelihood of early success, test the process, and build commitment and momentum for more extensive changes.

STEP FIVE ACTION ITEMS
CREATING A WORKABLE PLAN

1. Define where we are (WWA) now, specifically in terms of economics, competitive position, employee performance, future expectations, and the like.

2. Identify where we want to be (WWWTB) after the breakthrough change, with as much of the same specificity (from item 1) as possible.

3. There may be several possible WWWTB outcomes. Engage the team in dialogue about this. Consider outside resources to help you think this through. Consider ways to preserve optionality as you get into the project and see how things are developing.

4. Define the parameters for what constitutes success and failure, and frame these parameters in terms of relevant context: economic/financial outcomes, competitive position, and growth prospects. Think in terms of what outcomes you are optimally shooting for and what would be minimally acceptable.

5. Now develop the key milestones for how do we get there? (HDWGT). You will celebrate these deliverables as key successes; you should have major milestones you can celebrate at least every six months. These are the milestones you will communicate across the organization.

6. Identify the high-level tasks that are needed to achieve each key milestone. Given the task plan you develop, are the high-level milestones scheduled in item 5 achievable? If not, make adjustments.

7. How much money will be needed, both in terms of expense and capital? Add a substantial cushion for unknown problems and setbacks.

8. If there is a huge degree of uncertainty, consider stage-funding the effort. Identify key milestones or points where future funding decisions will be reviewed.

9. What return can you expect from this change over five to ten years? (Note that this return might not be financial.)

10. What other resources will be needed (people, space, IT, and so on)?

11. What key risk factors might you encounter? (See Chapter Ten for more details on this.)

12. Develop a plan to mitigate each of the risk factors identified in item 11. Consider how you might use biweekly steering committee meetings and a defined issue escalation process to help.

13. Develop two additional plans:
    a. An ongoing communications plan for Step Three
    b. An ongoing plan for the leadership team to review periodic results, evaluate, and adjust

6

Step Six: Partitioning the Project and Building Momentum with Early Wins

Far-reaching change initiatives can be hard for people to visualize, particularly if the gap between here and there, between the present and the future seems extraordinarily large. Change itself is hard enough, but a change that seems abstract and far in the future is even more difficult to grasp. Leading breakthrough change often means working toward an end that seems distant and out of focus. As we saw in earlier steps of the Stacking the Deck process, if your people can't visualize the future in real terms, they'll find it difficult to muster the urgency to undertake the journey.

You have to be committed to your ultimate goal, and you must be able to make that goal crystal clear, even when it may still seem impossibly distant, abstract, or even obscure. It's relatively easy to get everyone all fired up in the beginning; the greater challenge to your leadership is keeping spirits high even as the project stretches on. To lead breakthrough change successfully, you therefore need ways to make the immediate steps clear and to help people—particularly those who may not have been involved in developing the vision but who will be crucial to its realization—see the path to the future in real, concrete terms.

Stacking the Deck is all about preparing ourselves and our people to successfully undertake the change initiative. It's a process, and the less threatening, more compelling, and more achievable you make this process, the more likely you are to meet with success. We've previously discussed the importance of creating and maintaining momentum as we work through the often long and arduous process of implementing breakthrough change. The value of the detailed, long-range planning undertaken in Step Five cannot be overstated. The strength and detail of that plan will help you get people on board and mobilized. In this chapter we look at ways to partition the initiative to build in successes, support the bottom line, and keep everyone engaged over the long haul of breakthrough change.

PLANNING FOR INTERIM SUCCESSES

One of the best ways to preserve the enthusiasm that you have generated early on is to divide a major breakthrough change initiative into smaller phases, having shorter and intermediate-term goals with specific, clearly defined benefits. Partitioning the change initiative into smaller goals creates a "one step at a time" approach that feels more manageable and thus easier for individuals to commit to. Ideally, each of these smaller goals will take less than twelve months, preferably six months or less. They provide a series of checkpoints where you can celebrate interim successes on the road to a completed change. Initiatives that lack major deliverables in intervals of less than twelve months are much riskier to attempt, in part because it's extremely difficult—financially and emotionally—to wait beyond twelve months for a hint of success. Without at least a few interim successes, you run the risk of dissipating your team's momentum and energy.

As a number of leaders stressed, planning for interim successes has multiple benefits. By delving into the details of a phased approach, you can uncover issues well before they turn into problems. All too often, as Citi's Debby Hopkins points out, "the quality planning that would be required to break things up into a phased approach is simply missing, and the project suffers as a result." Instead she recommends taking the time to "think about your plan in more detail up front. Doing so makes every other part of it easier—and makes for fewer surprises down the road."

Taking the time to plan in detail, dividing a large-scale plan into increments, enables you to anticipate and time each phase and measure the core deliverables that indicate success. Breaking a change initiative into a phased approach improves the quality of planning and, in the long term, can also make you a better, more detailed planner.

It also enables you to show results and increase support for the initiative. Without a phased approach, without partitioning your project, you run the risk of employees, team members, or those you report to simply losing faith in the project. If you are aren't producing results—positive results—top management may begin to allocate fewer resources to the project. Cutting back may make sense from their perspective, because without seeing positive results, they may be left feeling they are throwing money at a black hole. It's not pretty when time, resources, and people go into a project and no tangible benefits come out. With careful planning, partitioning enables you to show results on a regular basis.

As we've seen in other steps, when you're leading breakthrough change the work of selling your vision of the future is never really done. In a very real way, you and your team must constantly pitch your change initiative and constantly justify its existence. You have to provide evidence that you're on the right path. Visible, measurable evidence of success can help you overcome the naysayers and is a very potent tool in your arsenal. Progress reports are helpful, as are completed tasks, but the actual interim deliverables that bring interim benefits to the company are most successful in building and maintaining project momentum. As Renée James at Intel notes: "Cultural inertia works against you when you have a whole lot of people looking for evidence of failures. To counteract that, you always have to provide evidence, you have to convince, convince, convince." There's no denying that "convince" is a key word when it comes to finding and developing interim successes.

Build In Celebrations

"Celebrate" is another key word for the team and the overall plan. It does no one any good to let a success, including a small interim success, slide under the radar unnoticed. Without a sense of accomplishment and achievement within the team, burnout can become a problem. Acknowledging and celebrating small, staggered successes boosts morale and helps with team retention. From both a career and psychological perspective, people need to be seen to have accomplishments. Further, each celebration can reinforce the overall goal. Particularly if that goal is far on the horizon, you should create small celebrations in all phases of the initiative.

In discussing the challenges of moving through a long-range change, Renée James emphasized the vision and the need to stay energized, to have endurance. She brought up the twenty-mile march that Jim Collins wrote about in *Great by Choice*: "We're going to go twenty miles down this road, and next year we're going to go twenty miles more, and the year after. Five years from now we're going to be in an entirely new place." Renée understands that "in the days, months, and years it will take to get there, people get fatigued. You have to keep energizing your team." Looking back, she realizes that in comparing successes and failures the difference for her "has been in how pragmatic the bridge and bridging strategy were. How did we translate the current activity into forward momentum? After two years of progress toward the goal, we want our people to wake up and think: 'We're a different organization now!'"

When Howard Schultz stepped back into his former role as chief executive officer of Starbucks in 2008 (after eight years as its chair), he knew there was much to be done. This was in the depths of the financial crisis, when Starbucks' financial future was particularly bleak, and Howard understood they were going to have to make significant cuts and tough decisions in order to save the company. He knew everyone needed to be on board and focused on the right goals and values for the business to turn around and thrive again. And convincing everyone involved would take some significant effort.

As Howard told me, "If you are a Starbucks store manager, you know how many stores and millions of customers there are. You might even begin to believe that whatever you do doesn't matter as much because the company is so big." But he knew that the mentality of language, purpose, and culture do matter—a great deal. He also knew that getting people to believe and having them be all in is critical, that "you can't achieve bold change if there are people within the organization who are doubting the intent and don't feel as if they're part of the idea or the solution, the tactic and, ultimately, the decision." In creating a plan to reinvigorate Starbucks, he stressed being "personally accountable and that every single customer, every single transaction, every single interaction matters more than at any other time."

It took some convincing for people to understand just how real the threats were to the company's survival. Ultimately, as Howard explained, "We had to reframe our thinking and say, 'It's not millions of customers a week. It's one customer at a time.' And that's something you as a manager feel you can control." Working with that thought, Starbucks used "a very basic arithmetic that we shared with the managers. If every store manager in the company added five more customers a day, at the average sale of $5 and multiply that by the number of stores we had, think of the difference it could make to our business!"

As Howard described more thoroughly in his book *Onward: How Starbucks Fought for Its Life without Losing Its Soul*, once people understood and were thoroughly convinced of the need for change, they began to turn the company around. Starbucks started celebrating every new customer. They also started sharing that information with the field operations every single day—and still do. Through all their efforts, Starbucks is reinvigorated and is now actively innovating for the future.

None of those improvements were by accident or by luck. They required a detailed plan and active involvement. Convincing partners (employees) of the need and then celebrating the interim successes—the new and returning customers—helped to build the needed momentum.

Turn to the Customer

Howard was quick to point out that he views the need for change and innovation as "two parallel tracks. One is customer-facing and one is partner-facing. To create significant customer-facing change innovation you need your company culture to be such that people want to make that kind of effort." To turn the company around, he understood that "we first needed to restore the trust and confidence within the culture and values of the company. You can't succeed and build a great enduring company unless you are deep in understanding that the culture drives everything. Everything. And to create bold change that endures you must focus on both the customer-facing initiatives and the partner issues in parallel."

It's all too easy to fixate on the people who are most immediately vital to your project: your team members and your management. Certainly they demand much of your focus. But as Starbucks learned, the customer is even more important and needs even more attention. Without customers, your change initiative may never make it to completion, no matter how groundbreaking and positive it is in theory. If you've recently lost customers, you need to quickly determine why and focus attention on their needs, perhaps by first attending to a part of the overall change initiative that will bring them back. In fact, large changes often come out of some sort of deficiency in the way that your organization is serving the customer. While you're working to correct that deficiency, remember that customers are still experiencing the old way of doing business; you may need to create an improved method of serving them in the interim. You could pull someone from the team to problem-solve, but bringing in an outside expert may get you to the answer quickly and smoothly, and without taking a team member's time and focus.

Fred Matteson joined Schwab in 1996, fresh off a senior technology position at Morgan Stanley. Today he is a partner at Alvarez & Marsal Business Consulting. In 2012 he visited my Executive MBA class to share his experiences and insights. He had been consulting for an insurance company that had sky-high goals, and he inherited a very aggressive initiative that required a totally revamped project approach to be successful. Known primarily as an online insurance provider, the company also does a great deal of business over the phone. But as Fred explained, "Their cost per call is high and they believed many aspects of their phone-based business needed revamping. When we looked at it, we found that resequencing the project phases and putting a few simple changes up front could have a huge impact on the economics and the project momentum."

Fred described three areas of change and the impact they had. "They needed to change their call tree to put the self-service options up front." Doing so enabled callers to immediately access all customer options (such as sales, service, and checking their account balance). Customers couldn't pay bills online unless they were past due. Why? "There was no valid reason—other than the fact that it had been programmed years and years ago and no one had ever reevaluated." He learned that "many requests that people call for could easily be done on the web. But the company's website had a large, obvious customer service number in the top right corner. So what do people do? They call." Fred explained that for "most web-oriented material, you want to bury the customer service number just a little bit. It shouldn't be ridiculously hard to find. But you want to give people opportunities to explore your website and maybe find a way to solve their problem without having to call."

These straightforward fixes "cost very little money to do." By implementing them, the company "lowered the number of nonproductive calls, drove more self-service, and reduced call handle times. That will free up capacity and save money for them to invest in the more strategic changes they need to do that will take a couple of years."

The changes that Fred implemented for his client are perfect examples of finding interim successes while creating value for the customers at the same time. Anything that streamlined the call center process made life easier for customers. Efficiency is not just a positive for the company's bottom line: customers want efficiency as well. And the goal in all of this is greater customer delight and advocacy.

BUYING MORE TIME WITH INTERIM SUCCESSES

Even if you have management's support, you can always use interim successes to your advantage. With them, you can offer tangible value to the organization to ensure that support stays in place and that your team doesn't lose faith in the project. In the long run, it pays to constantly be on the lookout for small wins and low-hanging fruit, those small interim deliverables that can demonstrate progress, deliver concrete benefits, and prop up both team morale and management support.

Mike Bell has dealt for years with the complex and fast-paced tech market. He is the corporate vice president and general manager of the new devices group at Intel, having been on the executive management team at Palm Inc. and vice president of CPU software at Apple, where he helped bring out the initial iPhone. Mike well knows that as fast paced as tech is, products take years to go from conception to market. Interim successes and celebrations are critical to maintaining project momentum. He shared a story about a very complicated plan to roll out some new technology at Intel. "There were three basic problems that I was trying to solve. The first was a public perception that the technology was simply never going to work in this space, and that Intel was irrelevant. The second was our process for implementation was horribly broken from a hardware, a software, and a program management standpoint. And then the third issue, of course, was that at some point you wanted to make money in this space."

The question was how to prioritize these issues. Mike knew that "we would never make any money at all if we didn't get the basic implementation issues fixed. And if we didn't change public perception, we would never sell enough to make money. So I had three huge issues that were completely intertwined."

This required Mike and his team to go "back to basics to fix the whole implementation from the software and hardware up. We changed the way we did road maps and planned the chips to create a successful proof of concept. We used that success to combat the public perception that we weren't relevant in the mobile device market space. And we made sure we were ready for the trade shows and forums where the press and the analysts see who's who in the business and what is being done."

The trade shows were critical as places for Intel to show progress and ensure that "our product was well understood by the analysts and the press. When I first joined Intel, analysts and members of the press started every conversation by saying, in effect, 'It's well known your technology can't possibly go into a mobile device or a tablet. It's too big, too hot, too power hungry. What are you going to do to fix that?'" Counteracting that impression was key. Mike knew that "the most important thing at that point wasn't fixing the flaws in the technology, but demonstrating that it was even viable and relevant. Even the best technology is not going to sell itself, unless you show relevance to the customer base."

As part of his process, Mike "worked to align all of these steps to deal with the technology issue and the relevance issues at the same time. And then I could take the results of these changes and use them to solve our perception problems. Luckily, those changes were working, and they were highly visible. It's not enough to be good. We have to be the best, or we will be dismissed."

Mike described a partitioned approach to a very bold and difficult change initiative that will take five years or more to unfold. By dividing it and prioritizing the interim steps, he is able to move forward, to make progress that is measurable and that will support the overall success of the initiative.

––––––––––––––

Breakthrough change is often about a new way of doing business, a new distribution channel, a new product, a new position in the market. As you develop your plan, carefully consider which interim steps you will focus on first. How will you capture what you've learned from those steps and celebrate the interim successes? How will you increase and maintain momentum? How will you fund it all?

If you follow the steps of the Stacking the Deck process, you will be able to anticipate potential delays and prepare yourself and your team for surprises, both of which could add expense and time to the project. Further, sometimes in the process of instituting breakthrough change, you have opportunities to cut costs along the way. This may not be something you set out to do at the beginning of the project, but as you move forward the benefits become clear. When a situation like this arises, you should take full advantage of it. Be sure to quantify the benefit. You can then essentially reinvest in your own project, using the money you've saved or produced with these smaller, incremental changes.

This brings us to our next step, in which we explore the topics of measurement, metrics, and analytics and their key role in supporting the overall plan and reinforcing support for the initiative, both of which must be done continuously.

STEP SIX ACTION ITEMS
PARTITIONING THE PROJECT AND BUILDING
MOMENTUM WITH EARLY WINS

1. Partition your plan into phases and subphases. Do your best to ensure each phase has a major milestone approximately every six months. (See Step Five, item 5.)
2. In addition to the big visible end goal everyone is aware of, which of the key milestones in your plan (from Step Five) can you celebrate as important interim successes toward the larger and longer-term vision?
3. Identify the project team members who are accountable for these milestones and make sure they are visibly associated with its planned achievement.
4. How will you communicate and celebrate these successes? Give specific examples. Remember that it's more about recognition and gratitude than money. Celebrations will have broad participation.
5. Who on the team is responsible for developing the celebration and communication of key successes? Different milestones may have different celebration leaders.
6. If the initiative will impact customers, how can you make the customer impact visible and tangible to the employees to further inspire them? Have fun with this and don't be afraid to be a little hokey: it's supposed to be fun and celebratory.
7. This isn't a "one and done" event. Breakthrough change can often be a long, drawn-out affair. Look for ways to celebrate milestones and achievements along the way to maintain momentum and morale.
8. Are there opportunities to "capture and harvest" short-term wins and economic benefits in the project's early stages? Capture, quantify, and communicate as appropriate.

7

Step Seven: Defining Metrics, Developing Analytics, and Communicating Results

The Stacking the Deck process is all about strategies, techniques, and approaches we can use to make our breakthrough change initiative successful. We also need to consider and specifically define what we really mean when we say "success." For while you are determining what success with respect to the initiative means for you, everyone around you will be doing the same thing—and possibly reaching different conclusions.

KNOWING YOUR KEY RESULTS

To define success for your initiative you need to focus on measurable outcomes. Without that, you run the risk of not being absolutely clear about the goals; as a result, people may have vague or differing ideas. Instead they need to see the end result with such clarity that they can act on their own.

I spoke with Marcus Nicolls, senior vice president of Partners In Leadership Inc., a firm that has helped thousands of companies worldwide improve teamwork and create a Culture of Accountability®—that is, a culture in which everyone at every level is focused on the vision and the key results the organization has established as its goal. The scenario he described—one in which "your people, at every level of the organization, self-select appropriate actions that deliver the desired result and take accountability to think and act in the manner necessary to achieve the key results"—is one leaders strive for, and one that can ease and speed the path to success.

What are your key results? Marcus advises distilling this down to "the top three or four most important deliverables, as a company. Doing so helps create the unity and team mind-set essential to alignment and ownership for the outcome." Not coincidentally, doing so also helps avoid the "Not My Job" pitfall. As he explained, a key result "is not your mission, vision, or values, but it does measure how we're doing toward accomplishing those bigger-picture objectives." He followed up with a warning: most leaders think they are clear about results. Often they feel they talk about the desired results so much that people must have memorized them. In speaking of this dilemma, Marcus quoted the Partners In Leadership Workplace Accountability Study: "Nine out of ten executive teams cannot uniformly articulate their top three key results and exactly how they're measuring them." Pausing for effect, he then added, "And that may be an underestimation!"

He described an interaction with a general manager who when asked, readily detailed the top three results and the exact metrics needed for the coming year. When asked, "What percentage of your executive team will give me the same three results and the same metrics?" the manager replied, without hesitation, "Oh, it'll be high—80 percent. It better be! I've been GM here for two years and I talk about these all the time." When all nine members of the executive team were then interviewed, "no two of them described the same list with the same metrics. Despite the GM's confidence that the team was well aligned and working on the same results, there was significant misalignment." If this executive team is so far out of kilter on the top three most important results, "imagine how misaligned the rest of the organization was."

Marcus sees this type of disconnect and misalignment as a big problem, but one that can be readily resolved by focusing on key results. The company's philosophy boils this down into simple guidelines: "Key results should be meaningful, measurable, and memorable. Meaningful suggests they are written broadly enough that everyone can link to them. Measurable speaks to one simple number that quantifies the goal line. There are many metrics to track, but simplicity is required at the top when it comes to what's most important. Memorable speaks to simplicity—your people won't take ownership for results they don't remember!"

To be clear, just reiterating your key results will not get you there. Much as the six blind men in the Indian parable experience and describe the elephant on the basis of where they stand and which part of the elephant they touch, until you share information together you cannot have a true sense of the reality in front of you.

WHAT ARE YOU MEASURING?

There's a strong desire in business to measure everything with one simple question: how much money are we making right now? This is perilous thinking, however, because financial performance in the early steps of a project is rarely the best way, and certainly not the only way, to measure success. When we are making a breakthrough change, the end goal of enhanced profitability could be a long time in coming. There are always other more immediate factors we can track that will lead to profit improvement down the road. And when that road is long and uncharted, as it often is with breakthrough change, it's particularly important to measure the interim steps and goals along the way.

As a rule, Citi's Debby Hopkins said, "people behave as they are measured. And if they're all measured by quantitative goals such as how much revenue you put on the board, they might discount a larger, more innovative project. Being able to evaluate people on their ability to form interesting teams and demonstrate creating a range of possibilities changes the game." An advantage here, as Debby explains, is that "you can create a range of opportunities rather than simply incrementally move from where we are to a little bit better place."

However, something else must come first, Debby says. You must "first help people understand the bolder idea—and the fact that with this idea, we have to think about goals differently. Yes, we're still going to have goals, we're still going to be transparent, and we're still going to be accountable to those goals. It just won't be in the same way as when you put an incrementally changed product out there. If, for instance, you're going after an idea that is new to the market, the goals must be different."

When I undertook the branch network changes at Schwab, I did think that making our branches more customer-oriented would eventually increase profits for the company. And "eventually" was a key word there. But if you had asked me what my goal was at the outset, I would have said something about a more efficient and effective branch network that would better serve our customers, build customer loyalty, and increase the percentage of their investments (the "share of wallet") that customers would entrust us with. The kind of all-encompassing changes that were necessary here demanded something other than a strictly bottom-line approach.

Debby and I discussed the issues of budgeting and numbers-driven approaches, coming back to the importance of understanding what drives behavior (that of customers and employees) and what drives results. She concluded by saying, "We see organizations that spend an insane amount of time doing bottom up, top down planning, budgeting, and analysis multiple times, when instead it would be more effective to first have a broader debate about what the answer should be and what it is going to take to get there."

The tug-of-war between senior leaders (or boards) who always want aggressive goals and "more for less" versus change leaders who try to determine what they realistically need and then add a cushion or a margin for error may well predate the Pharaoh and his lead pyramid construction engineer. What Debby is suggesting instead is that we focus on and debate the future we are shooting for, how we would measure and define that success, and what that success would be worth to our organization. Having those discussions early will help us more clearly frame what it will take to get us there and whether that level of resource commitment and risk burden is merited. I could not agree more. This kind of heartfelt discussion is healthy—and not practiced often enough.

MEASURING PROGRESS AND SUCCESS: BIG DATA, METRICS, AND ANALYTICS

The goals for change, particularly for breakthrough change, can often seem subjective and nebulous, especially to managers and operators. The leaders and high-level executives who are responsible for funding a given project want concrete, measurable indicators that tell them how a change is going. Historically, the usual word attached to these kinds of indicators has been "metrics."

Way back in the early eighties, those of us in direct response marketing measured and analyzed everything we could. In that world, success was the difference between a response rate of 1.5 percent versus 2.5 percent. And determining how much of that came from which part of marketing and promotion—new advertising, new slogans, new positioning, new product features—was something we were constantly trying to test for and measure. But the rise of big data since the turn of the century has changed all that, and now the sheer depth and breadth of variables we can collect, track, measure, and analyze means that organizations big and small are trying to figure out their strategy for leveraging this newly available and increasingly affordable resource.

Big Data

The possibilities big data offers seem phenomenal; the opportunities to analyze enormous amounts of data in real time, very enticing. But what are the practicalities? How should leaders factor big data's potential into breakthrough changes they're rolling out today? A *New York Times* article by Gary Marcus and Ernest Davis entitled "Eight (No, Nine!) Problems with Big Data" (April 6, 2014) pointed out many of the problems with big data, including the ways it can be gamed and distorted, and how errors can easily be magnified even as the terms used give "the appearance of exactitude." And yet, as they write, "Big data is here to stay, as it should be."

In contemplating the question "Does big data give a real advantage?" I talked with Asurion's Steve Ellis, who described big data as "a transformational trend, not just in the business world, but in society more broadly." He spoke of how he'd love to have "a dashboard with real time figures showing status on a full range of metrics"—and he understands that can take years to get in place. If you need to build a big data capability as part of a change effort, Steve believes "the time and resources required to get there can overwhelm the project if you're not careful," particularly so in an older company. Often, older companies still rely on legacy systems with more limited amounts of data stored in databases that are tough to access. Typically, their technologies were built before storage and processing power were as amazingly inexpensive as they are today. In contrast, younger companies have often built or rented technologies that include data warehouse capabilities and cloud computing infrastructure to capture, store, and analyze huge amounts of data. Those companies in which big data capability has already been built in therefore have a distinct advantage, one that Steve likened to "driving a well-tuned Corvette when your competitor is still having a tough time getting his old Chevette subcompact out onto the road."

While you may have ready access to elements of big data that can be useful and easily tapped, in many cases adding a big data construction project onto the fundamental change initiative you are undertaking is a trap to be avoided. Building big data capabilities is a major change project in and of itself, and your project is undoubtedly challenging enough. Whether your company is new or old, Steve was clear that you must "be very disciplined, targeted, and pragmatic in what data you go after, so that the data you gather is manageable." Steve suggested that "the most important process is understanding what the three to five most important metrics are, the leading indicators, that have the highest correlation to the outcome you're after." Then invest the time to create real-time monitoring of "metrics that matter." His final comment was clear: "Big data is an immensely powerful competitive weapon, but like any weapon, it needs to be aimed at the right target."

After my conversation with Steve, I spoke with Jim Hornthal, cofounder and chairman of Zignal Labs, a big data analytics company that effectively rents solutions to companies that are unable to build these solutions on their own. He offered an alternative approach, recalling that many of us "grew up in a world with a 24-hour news cycle. Reading morning newspapers and clippings services was the best we could do to understand changes in the marketplace to allow leaders to refine their positioning and strategies." In today's world of social media and hyper-fast digital information dissemination, "managing effective change often requires leaders to keep their fingers on the rapid pulse of dynamic, ever-changing data. While the prospect of constructing big data solutions can be quite daunting, we have seen Fortune 50 companies gain significant operational and strategic insights from big data with limited investment, opening their eyes to the real-time dynamics with their markets, customers, suppliers, and competitors." Jim believes big data analytics is critical and that useful solutions can be rented rather than built.

Even as capabilities evolve, it's clear that given the changes brought by big data, the traditional terms of metrics simply don't go far enough. Instead, we need to think in terms of analytics as we strive to use the newly available data most effectively. Charts and graphs now exist on TV monitors and can be updated in real time. Other approaches to data visualization need to be considered as a critical part of the monitoring and analytics process. Additionally, new tools such as "word clouds" and "heat maps" are powerful ways to look at data that would otherwise be difficult to digest and end up as "noise" rather than insight. (Sample word clouds and heat maps are shown on this book's website.)

How do we best make use of the data and monitor the indicators? There are two major types of indicators—leading and lagging—each with different implications for your breakthrough change initiative. Often indicators are analyzed simply by comparing current numbers to prior numbers. While period comparison and trending analysis can offer useful information, that information can be overly simplistic. For deeper, more thorough analysis, vintage and ratio analysis can provide valuable information.

Leading Indicators

As the name implies, leading indicators are harbingers or evidence of success or failure that appear before any of the others. It's a common misconception that market share and profitability are leading indicators. In fact, it's more likely that we are hoping these will dramatically accelerate toward the end of the project; they rarely do so at the beginning.

For example, if we've started rolling out a new web-based service, leading indicators might be represented by how many hits the website has received, how many people have logged in to the service, or how this data is trending over time. This information gives a sense of whether or not we're attracting new or existing customers with our website and whether we are getting the customer engagement that we want. We could also look at staff turnover. Did anyone quit last week? Last month? Last quarter? If so, how many and what did they describe as their reasons? This information can tell us how employees are adjusting to the change. These variations occur as a direct and immediate result of the changes we are implementing. We can measure these along with a host of other factors and follow their trends over time.

We also need to pinpoint the leading indicators to clearly and proactively articulate the targets for each one to management and to employees. Then, with those clarified, it will not appear that we are trying to justify any lagging profitability results down the road.

The following list sets forth leading indicators you might consider measuring. Bear in mind that there are many potential leading indicators to track; too much data may overwhelm people and dilute the focus of your group's efforts. Choose your indicators carefully, based on the nature of the project.

1. Measures of customer engagement such as customer calls or log-ins, click-throughs to deeper parts of your website, visits to physical locations, and purchases of various merchandise lines or products.
2. Measures of employee engagement, attitude, and turnover.
3. Trend lines revealing how key indicators move over time periods.
4. Customer loyalty as measured by online recommendations, endorsements, referral programs, or by the Net Promoter Score.

5. Sales numbers, units, dollars, average price, product mix.
6. Public relations as measured by number of positive mentions and numbers of headline stories, product reviews, or articles about your product or initiative, as well as social media mentions in tweets, retweets, and the like.
7. Share of customer "wallet," meaning the percentage of all the purchases customers make in your product category. What share of those purchases are you capturing?
8. Number of revisions to the expected final outcome of the project, and the percentage change.
9. The rate at which you are adding new accounts or customers.
10. Any cannibalization of an existing product with a new product launch. It is critical that the two factors (old product, new product) be linked together in the analysis.
11. Customer complaints, by type and number.
12. Any customer attrition you may experience.

Keep in mind that some of these indicators can potentially be lagging indicators as well, depending on the situation. For example, customer attrition may be a leading indicator in the sense that it's a problem you want to see beginning to decline as your new initiative takes hold. However, it can also be a lagging indicator since a new service or pricing approach may cause customers to leave, either because they are regrettably priced out, or by design because the company's focus is on higher-potential customers.

You will be measuring leading *and* lagging indicators, simultaneously, from the start of the project. Initially, the lagging indicators create the baseline to measure against as new trends eventually emerge. Your expectation is that the leading indicators will move first in the positive direction you are hoping for. You don't really know when the lagging indicators will begin to improve, although your project plan and economic forecast will require you to make a guess. Until the lagging indicators start to go up, people may be on pins and needles, nervous about results; you must be the voice of confidence and reassurance to keep morale high. The time lapse between positive trends in leading indicators and clearly improved results in lagging indicators can certainly be months and quarters if not even years. If leading indicators are disappointingly low, that same problem will likely be reflected in the final outcomes. Effectively measuring, tracking, and responding to the leading indicators are therefore critical.

Lagging Indicators

Lagging indicators are the big and important measures of success— such as reduced costs or improved market share, competitive position, pricing power, profit dollars, and profit margins—that we are working toward. Everyone wants to see positive lagging indicators and, typically, the sooner the better. But the results reflected in lagging indicators take time, sometimes years, to emerge. They are almost always foreshadowed by positive trends with leading indicators.

One of the great issues here is the difficulty of cultivating patience. There is huge pressure to see movement in the lagging indicators, no matter what the leading indicators are doing, and this pressure comes from everywhere: Wall Street analysts, stockholders, boards, senior management, you name it. eBay's John Donahoe and I spoke about this problem and how, even when the leading indicators are positive, it can be difficult to move forward without any encouraging movement in the lagging indicators.

"The financials tend to lag the reality," John began. "Just as the financials can look positive for a long period of time until suddenly the bottom drops out, the same thing can happen on the upside, where the actual lagging indicators that will give clear evidence of success take longer to come than you might feel that they should. Then you've got to focus on some of those leading indicators." John spoke from experience. "Early on in my situation at eBay, it was about trying to find little examples of where we had done what was right for our customer. I was looking for anything to indicate that we were doing the right thing in principle. We were making sacrifices during this time for the good of the customers. But we may not have been able to prove it yet, in the sense of having the metrics or the lagging indicators."

The wait for results can seem interminable. John explained that "it took about a year before those lagging indicators started to move. Despite all our work, there was just nothing to see. But whenever customers said something like, 'I noticed this little change you've made and I appreciate it' it gave us something to hold on to. It's not quantifiable, but it does tell us something. We had two years of really working hard and then only seeing the leading indicators improve incrementally."

It is a long, arduous process, which John didn't deny: "This is the Heartbreak Hill part of the turnaround. It's very easy to feel down: you're working hard and the finish line remains out of sight. Sometimes you just have to power through. If you're lucky, you do begin to see where you're improving the lives of your customers. But waiting for the financials to reflect your change and success is where character and tenacity really get built."

How do we help our people through that long period before the lagging indicators move? Yes, we have to power through, as John said. And that is helped enormously with analytics and measurements: the more precise and granular, the better. We want monthly, weekly, and even daily measurements. We want to see every emerging trend, and every reporting period counts. All this information can be used to help us make progress.

Vintage and Ratio Analysis

In comparison to leading and lagging indicators, *vintage analysis* is used less frequently. It is very powerful and immensely enlightening, and I believe it should be used more. With vintage analysis, one compares the performance of groups, or cohorts, of customers or employees to the performance of other groups over equivalent lengths of times in their gestation with the company. It is therefore a more sophisticated measure than simple year-over-year analysis. For example, you could compare the initial quarterly performance of all the sales executives who were hired and trained in the first quarter of *this* year with the initial quarterly results of those hired and trained in the first quarter of the *previous* year. Is this year's cohort (say the first-quarter hires of 2014) doing better or worse than last year's (the first-quarter hires of 2013), this then being at the same stage of their maturity in the business? If you have a major project and you need to train and reward the sales staff in new and different ways, then track and review their performance by vintage. This will let you answer the question, "Are the new sales executives hired this year who were on-boarded with the new training and rewards structure performing better in their first year on the job than the folks we hired a year ago before this structure was in place?" This allows you to definitively answer the question, "Is what we are doing differently working, adding value, and worth the effort and cost?"

We can also look at customers in this same way. If we consider every quarter's batch of new customers as a distinct cohort, or vintage, we can compare the characteristics of customers having equivalent levels of time with the company. Since customer life cycles are critical to most company's success, this kind of analytic is essential. Imagine we just instituted an entirely revamped process for acquiring new customers and introducing them to the broad range of services our company has to offer. In vintage analysis you might compare the first 12 months' totals for number of visits to our office, visits to the website, purchases of different products, or aggregate levels of revenues of (1) all customers who were first acquired in the first quarter of 2014 with (2) those newly acquired in the first quarter of 2013. Is the performance of the newer vintage better or worse?

Ratio analysis is an underutilized approach for measuring trends in business. In breakthrough change initiatives, we are hoping for significant trending improvements in outcomes versus inputs. But since the numbers are moving around so much, how should we analyze over various time frames? Ratios are an excellent way to do this. Obvious examples are sales per employee, revenues per customer or by customer segment, cost per lead, and close per lead. Also, you should be collecting data on measures of business (revenues, products purchased, new customers, and so forth) compared to website traffic and dollars spent to generate traffic. Essentially, you want to explore the relationship between inputs and outcomes over time and look for improving trends.

SHARING RESULTS—AND PROGRESS

We want the results that we're gathering to be highly visible so that everyone can see the progress as it is being measured and achieved. Progress posters and plaques on the wall may be old school, but they're still very effective. Now we can keep updates current on a video screen that employees see daily. In addition, we can make use of the digital possibilities: e-mail updates, phone updates, social media, tweeting. Make the analytics visible to the point of near inescapability. It's not always easy to do this, but it is always useful.

Early in my career, I was the marketing and business leader for the mortgage business in one of the Citibank regions. This was one of my first major leadership experiences, and I wanted to do everything I could to make my region (the highly competitive market of upper Manhattan) successful. In an attempt to get the lay of the land, I sat down with my boss and we ranked all of the regions. We based the rankings on new mortgage applications, new mortgages approved, delinquency rates, profitability, and other common markers of success. What did the numbers tell us? My region was ranked sixth. Not sixth out of fifty; six out of six.

Surprisingly, very few people in the organization really knew that. The executives knew, but the information hadn't yet trickled down to the people on the ground. How could they possibly appreciate the depth of the problem without some basic reference points? How could they have any sense of accountability if they had no way of measuring their work product against a competitive set of outcomes?

When those of us on the management team faced the facts, no one was satisfied with last place. So one of the first things we did was focus on the rankings described above and display our standings relative to the other regions. For this, we used four-foot-high poster boards. They were impossible to miss. Four of the categories were leading indicators; one, profitability, was a lagging indicator. We held executive team meetings and ultimately meetings of the entire staff to share our thinking, which included where we were, where the leadership team wanted us to be, and our improvement plan for getting there. The plan we set out was ambitious—and achievable. It was slow at first, but within a few months we very gradually began to climb up the regional rankings on some of the factors. Excitement and enthusiasm began to develop. I believe strongly that most people want to be winners, but for some the fear of failure is so great that they don't even want to try to do things differently. Those who were skeptics eventually became believers and started to pitch in. We had parties, gave away T-shirts and hats, and celebrated every time we moved up. Within less than a year we were number one in every ranking, and the entire team was enormously proud of what we had accomplished.

Let people know where they stand. The more visually powerful you make the display of information, the less team members can deny it. A good long look in black and white at one's performance can create a sense of urgency in a hurry. In addition to displaying how our region was doing, we used every opportunity to display how our individual staff members were performing. Some people who were near the bottom in our rankings were embarrassed by everyone knowing where they stood, but the intent was never to humiliate anyone. Over the years, we experimented with different approaches, such as only displaying the standings of individuals who were above the mean score of the group. But the facts are what they are, and we all have to be held accountable for our results.

My region had been ranked last not because it was full of terrible people, but because it was full of people who had neither challenged old ways of doing things nor looked for new processes and ideas, nor strived to meet a higher standard. The potential was there; we just needed a spark to get going.

It wasn't just the posters that made this happen. The spark was the leadership team standing before the employee group (about 100 people) and expressing our willingness to be held accountable for significantly improving our results, and our conviction that we could succeed. Even the most tenured of the managers committed to do things in new ways and to drive our rankings higher. We had to develop and implement real ideas for how to do things better—and we did. We instituted a major change in how mortgages were processed, under the rubric of "Mortgage Power." It included piloting the new idea of preapproved mortgages and creating a new, dedicated servicing desk for real estate agents. At first these innovations faced significant resistance internally. But as people began to see the logic and as the momentum from our success grew, so did the willingness of the team to do things differently, after having done them virtually the same way for decades. Employees were won over and this quickly became a memorable experience in which we were successful and had fun together.

Similarly, at Schwab, every branch office had big posters in the break room showing the performance of that branch versus the other branches in their region. Breakdowns charted the performance of each person relative to the others in the branch. Simply put, you can't have a good week until you have a good day, so it's important to have a clear sense of what you're accomplishing—or not—every day.

Be aware that making a change happen is deeply rooted in social and emotional issues. We are managing emotions. We are managing passion. We are managing people's energy and commitment to this breakthrough change—and it's a massive undertaking. It's very powerful to be able to take all that critical data and hang it up on the wall or on a video screen for everyone to see. Every day, an employee can come in and think, "I'm proud of my personal position," or "I need to work harder here." The leader's role in encouraging and guiding people to improve cannot be understated. As Dick Kovacevich, former CEO of Wells Fargo and ever the master motivator, said, "You have to inspect what you expect. You need to convince people that they can do better. And when they do their personal best, you need to celebrate it—in ways that make it clear that people's accomplishments are truly valued."

In addition to the numbers, we also want to celebrate and recognize the individual stories of personal sacrifice and commitment to the mission. These are the stories that people remember, and in telling these stories to the team, leaders have the opportunity to share their thinking with respect to movement in results and growing success. More important, by paying attention to and celebrating stories of personal sacrifice and commitment, we can genuinely demonstrate our gratitude to team members who are pouring their hearts and souls into our collective success, while we recognize and thank them for being role models for all of us. This is but a small piece of what we can do to manage emotions and passions, which is discussed more thoroughly in Chapter Eleven.

From leading and lagging indicators to big data to various types of analyses, the available information is nonstop. You need to determine what's most important among competing issues and direct your attention there. Often it will seem the only thing top management cares about is enhanced profitability—and in many ways that's true. But since breakthrough change almost always consumes capital for a long time before enhanced profitability emerges, this stretch can truly test your resolve. Remember that a narrow, myopic fixation on profitability alone can lead you to make rash course corrections and possibly have you heading off in the wrong direction. Prepare yourself; if the leading indicators are slow to move, you may need to use anecdotal stories to reinforce confidence and momentum. These stories, complete with detail, are typically dramatically more compelling than the statistics and can help the group persevere.

Remember that leading a breakthrough change is fundamentally about creating and managing both the actual momentum and the perception of momentum. As we measure and trend the leading indicators and as we are seeing some of the factors begin to move in the right direction, this movement needs to be acknowledged and celebrated. Ultimately, of course, the lagging indicators of growing profitability, margins, market share, and market position will need to make an appearance. But this can take years. In the meantime, having agreement on the leading indicators to shoot for, and measuring and celebrating them along the way, will build and maintain momentum for the change initiative among the larger team, which is discussed in Chapter Eight.

STEP SEVEN ACTION ITEMS
DEFINING METRICS, DEVELOPING ANALYTICS, AND COMMUNICATING RESULTS

1. What leading indicators will signal that the change initiative is producing early stage tangible business results?
2. What analytics could you use to measure progress against these indicators?
3. What lagging indicators will reaffirm that the change is (or isn't) working?
4. What analytics could you use to measure progress against these indicators?
5. Are the processes in place to capture, store, and access the data necessary to track and analyze the leading and lagging indicators in items 1 and 3 above? If not, what can you afford to build as part of this project to capture this data?
6. Which of these indicators can you measure and report on daily, weekly, monthly, and beyond?
7. Define where you want to be in relation to the leading and lagging indicators at given milestone dates (for example, a 10 percent increase in new customers n months out).
8. Are there big data initiatives in the company that you can tap into and employ?
9. Does vintage analysis aimed at customers or employees make sense for this project? What specific data will you analyze in this fashion over time? Do we have any data sources we can tap that will allow us to compare today's post-project vintages to older vintages?
10. What key ratios can be used to measure performance?
11. How will you communicate the status of the above indicators to the core change team and the broader organization (publish on home page, signage in office, and so on)?
12. Are any of these indicators critical to maintaining executive or board support for the project (for example, funding)? If so, how can you give that special attention?

8

Step Eight: Assessing, Recruiting, and Empowering the Broader Team

You have long since assembled and unified your leadership team. As discussed back in Chapter Two, you must accomplish this early in the breakthrough change process since your vision and plan for change will be far better if you have people with different perspectives, more skills, and a broad range of experiences at the table to challenge your ideas and offer additional ones. Typically, the early team needs to grow over time, both with new members for the leadership team itself and with new colleagues who may be one or more layers removed in the organization.

This chapter builds on the work you did in Step Two. At this point, you might want to revisit and repeat some of those initial team-building actions, for at least two reasons. First, it may be time to further strengthen the leadership team for the long haul. And second, as the focus shifts to bringing together the entire team, you need to attend to the broader team that will ultimately do all the heavy lifting to bring the change initiative to fruition. This means assessing skills, namely, skills that already exist within the organization, additional skills you will need to develop, and skills you will need to bring in. It also means recruiting for talent, fit, and balance, and empowering the larger team to succeed.

ASSESS TODAY FOR FUTURE NEEDS

This step also relies in part on the work you did in Step Five, as you began developing a long-range workable plan for your breakthrough change. Now it's time to update those assessments with an eye toward gathering and developing the broader team. Assembling a team with the skills that are known to be necessary and the flexibility and interest to grow into the unknown is a complex and demanding task. Like many other parts of the Stacking the Deck process, it's iterative; that is, you will need to return to it from time to time. And it is often more difficult in practice than we can accurately anticipate. Almost by definition, something as new as a breakthrough requires new skills—and often skills that haven't yet been broadly developed or even precisely defined.

IMAGINE THE DREAM TEAM—AND DREAM BIG

Even when you can't yet know all the specifics, you can start by dreaming big as you imagine your dream team. What would it take to make this breakthrough change happen within the time frame you've set and at the level you want? Given the scope of your breakthrough change and the talent you will need in your dream team, you will likely need to cast a broad net and look in ways and places that will bring your group diversity and strength in skills, experience, and track records. And if your change needs to happen quickly, your search needs to bring in top-notch people with the necessary skills right away.

Start with Diversity

When we think of the benefits of diversity, we often fall into the trap of defining diversity narrowly and focusing on its racial, gender, or ethnic dimensions. Recognizing that diversity strengthens a team's performance, we need to go even further and strive for diversity from every angle, especially including the less visible elements of attitude, experience, focus, perspective, and work style, as a few examples.

Keep diversity in mind for your dream team and for every iteration of the team. A team without diversity or a team that stays constant can get too comfortable. People can become so bonded with each other that they are unwilling to challenge one another meaningfully. Or even more destructively, groupthink sets in and suddenly the team doesn't have anyone with a divergent opinion—or anyone willing to voice one. Adding new people from new sources, inside or outside the organization, is a great way of keeping a team on its toes. Injecting new blood every few promotion cycles adds a new layer of challenge and opportunity. Since a constant influx of new members may mean the team will not gel in the way that more stable teams do, it's particularly important to monitor the team as it changes.

Schwab was changing so rapidly during my years there that I was constantly looking for new executives who could expand our team's experience, perspective, and skill. I consciously tried to maintain a promotion/recruitment ratio of 2 inside to 1 outside. If I was promoting someone from inside the company, I wanted it to be because they were able to contribute something special—the accumulated benefits of their experience and familiarity with the company. If I was recruiting someone from outside, it was because we were making a leap into something beyond our cumulative experience and we needed someone with the relevant background to help us through the change. The goal was to maintain a dynamic, multitalented group of people at the highest levels of the company. A team might include people who had been with Schwab for 15 years and others who had been there for 15 weeks, all working together successfully.

Integrating new people into a working team does present challenges, which you should not underestimate. You must constantly balance many variables. Do you have a team full of extroverts? Introverts? Leaders? Followers? Quick deciders, or more-reflective types? Just as you want to pull together a group of people who can work together productively, you also want to pull together a set of disparate experiences and skill sets that will mesh usefully.

Check Track Records

Common sense might suggest that you look exclusively for people with glowing track records, but that isn't always the best impulse. Ski instructors often tell beginners, If you're not falling, you're not learning. For the more advanced skier, If you're not experimenting with the edges, if you're not skiing on different types of slopes, you're not learning and practicing new skills. This doesn't mean that the most snow-covered student will ultimately become the best skier. But the comparison to skiing is useful as an analogy to remind us that unless we're willing to experiment and push toward the new, we won't continue to improve and reach the next level of challenge.

If a successful track record may thus have its downside, then in turn the person who has been involved with a failed project may well have gained priceless insight. In fact, one of the great upsides to a well-intentioned failure is the invaluable experience that people gain by having tried and failed. (The concept of Noble Failure is discussed more thoroughly in Chapter Ten.) If your goal is to never make the same mistake twice, it makes sense to broaden your database of mistakes and the learning that comes with those experiences as much as possible. By hiring someone from another organization who was integral to a project that failed there, you can acquire the lessons learned but without all the costs. Indeed, second only to a person's wealth of specific expertise, which you need, the next best reason to recruit from external sources is to learn from the mistakes people have made elsewhere.

Once you have imagined your dream team, you know what skills you need. And you know what kind of person you are looking for: an experienced innovator with a fresh perspective, who may have failed somewhere but who learned from that experience, and who is capable and excited about embracing change. The questions are then how you find the people you need and how you get them to join your team.

SEARCH FOR TALENT, SKILLS, AND FIT

You know that you're looking for people with precise skills, talent, and experience for your dream team. Now, where will you find those people? Given the nature of business, you may at first be limited to the people you already have available to you, those inside the organization. But what if there aren't enough people inside with the right skills? Or worse, there aren't any available? In a breakthrough change initiative, the chances are you will need to at least supplement the talent you have at hand and do so quickly.

Inside Your Organization

You will first want to look inside the organization to use the skills of the people you already know and trust, people who deeply understand the organization's mission and the importance of the breakthrough change. Being able to rely on people who are already part of the culture can be a tremendous boost.

This worked to our advantage at Schwab, time and again. In the early 1990s, when Schwab had decided to get into the mutual funds business in an entirely new way, we gave the assignment to Tom Seip, a devoted change junkie. Tom led an incredibly challenging effort to bring outside fund companies into the Schwab tent, and he succeeded. We moved Beth Sawi, former head of Schwab marketing, into the leadership role on our electronic brokerage business—and she transformed it into an industry-leading business. In moving the very capable John Coghlan from a job that poorly fit his skills and interests, we gave him the opportunity to blossom as he launched and then ran our Financial Advisor servicing business.

In each instance, we knew we had smart, capable executives who loved challenges. We knew they could recruit and lead exceptional teams and we gave them huge opportunities, which ultimately led to long-term competitive advantage for Schwab. They took the steep challenges, surrounded themselves with exceptional teams that blended inside talent with a smattering of outside talent, and they excelled. They have all moved on to new challenges and careers, but their contributions and legacies at Schwab continue to this day.

Insider Challenges Unfortunately, as leaders quickly realize, the reality they face within the organization is often quite different from these ideal examples. John Donahoe at eBay and I spoke about just this issue. As discussed in Chapter One, he too faced the challenge of needing a new skill set from a group of people who were wedded to the old ways of doing things. To be sure, difficulties do arise, but not just because of people's tendency to hold on to the past way of doing things. It's more than that. As John said, "It's also about a longing for the past. If people were part of something successful before, they naturally want to cling to that. They were winners once and they want to be winners again. But there's no guarantee that they have the commitment and tenacity that's going to be required to get to the new place. Or even that the new place will be as good as what they remember."

But there is no going back to the way it used to be. For those who have a tendency to look backward instead of forward, that idea is particularly difficult and all change is a challenge. John continued, emphasizing that some people are always measuring against history "rather than against the competitive environment, the customer needs, and all the other indicators we need to watch to succeed in the future. This comparison with the past is deadly because it's internally focused. It's too easy to fool yourself this way. Whether it's your golf swing, your marriage, or your business, if you're measuring exclusively against yourself, you get a distorted, less objective sense of how good you really are."

John nails it there. As they say in the financial industry, past success is not an indication of future performance. And in today's climate, the sentiment is true across all businesses and around the globe. In fact, a major success in someone's past can actually hobble that person when it comes to looking at change on the horizon. "Think of it," John said. "As some people grow their careers, they tend to become less and less comfortable with bold change. To them, bold change is how you build your reputation, not how you protect it." John talked more about how people become increasingly protective of their professional identities. "It's not even about how good or bad these people are at their jobs. A lot of the issue is context. The people who just couldn't get on board with some changes I had proposed moved on." He related that some of those people went to places where they hadn't been part of a past success and found they could embrace and even lead bold change. Perhaps that was because "they didn't have history there, and change or the avoidance of change wasn't all tangled up with their personal identity. Sometimes a move into a new scenario where people have to prove themselves again can shake them out of complacency and fear." We both understood that no one chooses to be ineffective. Many times a change of scenery can be the impetus that ultimately enables someone to be successful again.

Skill Gaps   All too often, when you embark on a breakthrough change initiative, you will discover that you don't have all the expertise you require right there at your fingertips. After all, it's only natural that employees focus their time and effort on becoming better at the processes and tasks the company has historically and habitually used. The very nature of breakthrough change upsets the comfortable order of the company and demands something new and daring.

If you've come to realize that even your best people are not right for the job, how do you go about finding the right people? This can be a long process, but one that you can shorten considerably by making a habit of looking out for talent and actively developing yourself as a talent magnet. If you have been consciously cultivating talented people both inside and outside of the organization, you already have a head start.

Becoming a Magnet for Talent

Ideally you want to be able to draw on an ever-expanding pool of talented people, both inside and outside your organization. If you want to engage the best of the best, you have to be extraordinarily compelling—not just in the compensation package you offer but in the personal experience you are inviting people to share. Part of this is simply being a good leader, someone people want to follow from project to project, someone who challenges people and draws out their best. If you are committed to being a leader of breakthrough change, the odds are good that you are going to have to assemble many teams over the course of your career. This makes it all the more important to create and cement connections with creative, talented, driven people, wherever they are. It requires being proactive and personal about building and maintaining your contact list, one step in the process of identifying people with skills or attitudes you may want on your team in the future.

Whether building a network comes easily to you or is a skill you need to work on, the sooner you start, the better. Consider the people you meet at a conference, people who have worked with you before, even people who have recently been part of high-profile change projects elsewhere. Keep tabs on these individuals and cultivate professional relationships with them. Stay in touch and take a personal interest, perhaps even offer to act as a mentor. The odds are good that you will both benefit. And someday you may need their unique talents on your team.

Drawing a Team to You Intel has long been the leader in the personal computer and data center server markets. However, their products had not been engineered for the fast-growing mobile markets of smartphones and tablets. These markets need lower-priced, lower-power technology, shorter development cycles, and experience as a scrappy, nimble competitor. Those of us on the Intel board and the leadership team understood that these distinctions changed everything about the skills and experience we would need as the company was developing new products; and they changed where we would need to look to find the right people.

When Mike Bell first joined Intel, he faced not only organizational tradition but pressure to recruit a team exclusively from within the Intel structure. Mike wisely ignored these suggestions, pointing out that Intel people may have had extraordinary skills and experience with PCs but did not know the mobile business. When Mike and I spoke about assembling a team and getting the right array of skills, he wholly agreed with the idea that context is critical for getting the best performance out of a team and he understood that "if you take great people and put them in the wrong roles, it's destructive. It hurts the effort and it really demoralizes and demotivates these people, who may have been superstars at what they did before. If you shove them into a place that they aren't suited for, it only does damage."

Instead Mike was careful and especially mindful about the people he brought together. In developing the mobile space at Intel, he searched for internal people who were not bound to the traditions and who were ready for new attitudes and skills. Well known as a magnet for talent, he ultimately found, in looking both inside and outside the company, "a mix of highly motivated, very smart people who had some relevant background, who had the right attitude, and who were willing to learn." As he said, "This mix of inside knowledge and outside knowledge is very powerful—and it needs to be properly balanced to be effective."

The insider-outsider dichotomy and potential synergy to which Mike alluded is only part of the story. When you are choosing your team members, you have to consider their personal history. People frequently get very comfortable after what might be years of success, and the successful track record that makes individuals desirable as team members can also make them too conservative and too concerned with protecting their legacies. As if that weren't enough, new people who are coming in from the outside will potentially be seen as "Mike's friends" and may be culturally rejected by the long-term base of the team. Creating a team of both insiders and outsiders has its own challenges for which a leader needs to be prepared. The benefits are certainly worth the challenge, but you shouldn't underestimate the time and effort this kind of team building requires.

Leaders who have a following are talent magnets—as Mike Bell clearly is—and the pieces seem to fall into place more easily as the team develops. As Mike said, "One of the key things I've learned over the years is that engineering is a team sport. In fact, some of the best things I've done in my career have been with a group of people I've worked with over the years, people whom I know and I can trust." When we spoke, Mike was in the process of assembling a team for a new project. He explained that "some people I know who are working for others have been calling me up and are asking to come on board. It's gratifying to see these people who have worked for me for years and they still want to come along and do something else."

A strong, solid team allows the whole project to move faster and perform better. It can make all the difference. But no matter what the team's makeup, we both understood that after teams have formed, they need tending and nurturing. Leaders "can't put a structure in place and then let it go," Mike said. Instead you need to constantly check in to be sure you have the right people, the right expertise, and that everyone's performing. This is particularly important when you're trying to move quickly. Being a personal magnet for talent is enormously helpful, then, both for the speed with which you can put together a team and for the ongoing quality and performance of that team.

You want to be someone who enables people to be their very best. That skill and ability to draw people to you reflects well on you and by the same token is something to look for in those you hire. Mike underscored this thought. "When I hire someone and then ask that person to build a team, if the response is something like, 'Oh, I wouldn't know who to hire,' I begin to get a little nervous. If a person doesn't have at least a small group of people to call and potentially bring over, that's a warning sign. Having a following is especially important these days." But what if you've already tapped all the likely candidates you know?

Recruiting Outside Your Network   Anyone who is looking forward to a long career as a leader should be establishing long-term connections, preparing for the future, and becoming a personal magnet for talent. But what if you find yourself in need of people who aren't yet in your network?

Mike offers some suggestions for finding and recruiting people: "After I exhaust my network of people, I rely on a couple of trusted recruiters who share my vision of how products should work and how people should work and we share a work-hard, play-hard philosophy. They know the quality of people I expect—and they are able to get these people interested and engaged enough to come talk to me. Then, I meet with these people face to face and see if they are a good fit for the team. Having that next level of network to find people is critical—and these recruiters have delivered time and time again." Naturally, you may have to try a few recruiters before finding one that works for you. When you do, Mike's advice is to nurture that relationship carefully, for doing so will save you time in the long run.

All of your efforts should work in concert to help build a highly capable team with the skill sets that you need. Over time, as you build your own reputation as a change leader, you become a more and more desirable boss. That, in turn, allows you to reach out even further and build more connections. Perhaps some of these people then come to work with you. If they have a positive experience and your work together is successful, then you've cemented your relationship, added depth to your experience, and bolstered your reputation. Ideally, your network of contacts and your reputation as a talent magnet then both expand still further.

UNIFY AND EMPOWER THE LARGER TEAM

No matter how strong you believe you are as a personal magnet or how good your recruiters are, don't underestimate the challenges of forging a cohesive team of insiders and outsiders, a team that is diverse and talented in a broad range of business aspects. Time and effort will be needed, both to create the team and to bring it together. The benefits of a strong team are worth it. And with the right team, creativity in the face of a crisis can work wonders.

Ginger Graham has run several businesses that focus on innovation and new product development and speed. She explained that at one point the medical device company she was then with, Advanced Cardiovascular Systems, was "woefully behind in stenting technology and losing market share in the core business because of it. So we formed what at that time was a quite novel, heavyweight team. We invited something close to 50 employees into a room for several days with a professional facilitator to map out how we had been developing products. Then we asked them to brainstorm and work together to answer the question, 'If you could change it all, if you could fix all the things that you believe the company has been doing wrong, what would that future development process look like?'" The group immediately set to work and redefined product development in the company. They defined a new way of developing products that would be "faster, leaner, more efficient, more focused—and that would allow us to catch up and win in the marketplace. We gave the team the resources they requested and wrote a contract with them about their deliverables with respect to product performance, product quality, time, and cost, and customer satisfaction and market performance on the results, based on them being able to drive product development as they believed it should be."

Bold moves brought breakthrough results, and as Ginger explained, "The employees did know more about how the work should be done and can be done, much more than those who managed it from afar." In fact, the process worked so well that the company "went from 1 percent to more than 75 percent market share on one product launch in a major category in stenting, when stents were still relatively new in this country."

Later, when that very success created its own problems, they went back to the employees for answers. Having launched a new variety of stent for use in heart surgeries in October, Ginger recounted that "before Thanksgiving, we faced product shortages. It's almost inconceivable that you could launch the market-leading product and be out of stock in such a short time frame. We did a global launch and we, as management, did all the calculations and all the number crunching."

Ginger described the questions they had to ask themselves: "Could we make enough to keep up since it's growing so fast? All of our numbers said no." So they had an all-employee meeting in each of the company's locations, during which "we showed them the response. We talked to them about what had happened with the launch, how the market had grown, and how many people needed our product." Ginger and her team brought patients and doctors in to talk about the product. They then asked the employees: "Is there a way that they could help us solve this? Is there any way we could produce more, faster?

"These employees told us, 'You need to help us with our Christmas shopping, you need to wrap our presents, we need babysitters, we need transportation. And we'll make it happen.' And they did.

"We held up our side of the bargain. We set up a giant wrapping station in the business and we wrapped everything imaginable.

We even wrapped a surfboard." Her stories of management volunteering to make life easier for these employees cover a wide range, from providing three meals a day to transportation for employees and for their children's babysitters. "As management, we had been sure that everyone would have to work both Thanksgiving and Christmas and worried that even so, we wouldn't make the numbers." Instead the company never ran out of product and *no one* had to work Thanksgiving or Christmas. "We put the future of this product in the employees' hands and they didn't let us down. It was an incredible personal experience for me and solidified my very strong views about how much employees drive the success of your business, not management."

Ginger's success stories of her empowered teams illustrate how much can be accomplished with the right teams and the right attitudes in place. It's a theme the leaders I interviewed returned to time and again. As Citi's Debby Hopkins said, "When you are leading a change, you must have a very acute sense of the team that you want around you. You are fighting insurmountable odds on so many fronts; understanding the types of people that you want to bring on board is a critical element. The team needs a sense of where we're going and a passionate belief to shore up that vision."

Passion is so important that, as Debby said, sometimes "it's tempting to think that passion is always the answer. But we also need people who are going to question that vision. If they're good questions—and if you as the leader have good answers—this will solidify your project." She refers to this aspect as "helping people 'step into why.' Why do we think this is a good opportunity? How do we get there? What are the components? These questions build a bridge that people can follow, a bridge that enables them to see across to the other side. So passion is great, but sometimes you also need some skepticism, that different perspective."

It may seem odd to think that skepticism can be helpful. But constructive skepticism can keep you from very enthusiastically driving over a cliff. And that same skepticism is invaluable as you keep the team fresh and thriving.

REBALANCE AND REVAMP THE TEAM

As with virtually every other Stacking the Deck step, assessing the available skills is not a one-time thing. You must constantly reexamine this careful balance between insiders and outsiders, between the old guard and new blood, between known and unknown quantities. To keep your team functioning, you must remain alert to what skills you and your team may lack and how well people are working together with the structure that's in place.

Sometimes even when you think your team is all set you will be surprised. In our early years at HighTower—a relatively new wealth management firm where I serve as chairman of the board—we thought we had assembled exactly the team we needed to go forward. The strength and experience of this team were critical to our ability to raise capital. However, as we got off the ground, we learned that several of our key hires didn't fit the culture and pace of an early-stage firm, although they had been quite successful previously in a more mature company. This mix was not something we could afford, as we really didn't have depth and backups for these roles. We had to face the reality, quickly make a change, and figure out how to fill the gap until the right new hires could be found. Waiting to see if things were going to get better, which was our first inclination, would just delay the action that we desperately needed to take. We handled the situation with the urgency it deserved and eventually found the replacements to take the company forward. While it was pure hell for a while, the right new employees accelerated our progress and have become a huge part of our growing success.

Discussing a recent Intel project, Mike Bell mentioned that he found out six months into it that "some of the people I had thought could step up and do the job were only comfortable doing business the way they always had done it. They just weren't the appropriate people for the project and I had to go back in and make further changes." He realized that "you really have to constantly have a feedback loop that says: 'Yes, this is the right thing to do and these are the right people and everybody's still performing.' You have to keep evaluating it, to make adjustments along the way."

The balance between being provided with sufficient feedback to give the leadership team the information they need and offering the people on the ground enough leeway to be creative and fully involved can be a delicate one. In speaking of a team that was putting together a major new project as we spoke, JetBlue's Dave Barger explained that "the team leading our project put together explicit rules of engagement that made very clear where they had authority and where their authority stopped, in terms of capital and otherwise. Whether it concerned design of the product or changes that could be incorporated after a decision had been made, these rules of engagement were very clear about who had what authority."

Dave has a weekly meeting with his Executive Leadership Team. He remarked that "every six weeks for the past year, we've had an update from this project team. This cadence and the clear rules of engagement made a huge difference. They knew when they were free to use their own judgment and when they needed our decision—and they didn't need it much. We had gone out of our way to get these passionate high-achievers on the team, and we didn't want to micromanage their work and risk suffocating their interest and creativity."

Because JetBlue was aiming for a differentiated project, one "that's not cookie-cutter like other airlines, but something different, something that's in keeping with the irreverence of the JetBlue brand, it meant ceding some control to the project team. We knew that we would have the opportunity to check in every six weeks; they knew that there was going to be this kind of briefing. We picked the team members to develop this project and we let them do that."

Dave's experience highlights a challenge that every leader faces: learning how to give up control and deciding how much control to give up. Dave understood that it would be a shame and a misguided use of energy to spend so much time building a strong, bright, skilled team and then hamper them with oppressive oversight. Between the rules of engagement and regular check-in meetings together, the project team and the leadership team kept the project on track and balanced, observing suitable levels of authority where they were most needed.

In speaking of how teams are best built and fine-tuned, Starbucks' Howard Schultz mentioned that he had Tony La Russa (currently a baseball executive with the Arizona Diamondbacks and a former World Champion manager of the Oakland Athletics and the St. Louis Cardinals) talk to his management team. Howard explained that Tony, who had by then been named manager of the year four different times, "said something that day that didn't initially play well to our people. He said, 'Not everyone deserves to be on the team.' He gave a couple of examples of players who were selfish and not team players. And he got rid of them."

Later, Howard talked to his team about Tony's comments at some length: "If you have people in this company who you know are not going to rise to what we need, then you have to ask them to leave because they're not going to be producing for us. Not everyone deserves to be on the Starbucks team."

Just as companies are hardwired to do what they have always done and maintain the status quo, many people think that leadership is about reducing conflict and maintaining an even keel. But really that's what *management* is about. *Leadership* requires challenging your people, because challenge is the antithesis of complacency and is its antidote. Challenge can shake people out of complacency and move them toward a better future.

As you've no doubt gathered by now, one of the underlying themes in the Stacking the Deck process is that the work never stops. Not only do you need to keep reaching for challenges for yourself; you also need to keep demanding that your team rise to each new challenge, whether it's one you've actively planned or one that the changing world has presented to you. This may mean bringing in someone from another company, or another industry. This may mean moving people who have been working in one area for years to a different task or venue. New challenges demand constant adjustment to make sure that everyone is contributing their best to the team as a whole. This means keeping yourself and your team healthy and dynamic, ready for the inevitable surprises, roadblocks, and new challenges that pop up on the road to breakthrough change.

Now you have your plan, your analytics, and your team. It's time to implement pilot tests of your breakthrough change, as Chapter Nine describes.

STEP EIGHT ACTION ITEMS
ASSESSING, RECRUITING, AND EMPOWERING
THE BROADER TEAM

1. Consider the skills and experiences identified as necessary in Steps Two and Four. Does the organization have all of these skills? If not, can you teach them in an appropriate amount of time?

2. Will you need new staff, contractors, or consultants? How many and with which specific skills?

3. Are all levels of leadership and authority on board with the potential need to recruit people from outside the organization in order to fill skill gaps?

4. Do you have the budgetary authority to acquire the necessary resources? Will you have to find the money via efficiencies or staff reductions to make room for new staff? If so, what problems might this create?

5. Are there internal people who have been involved in breakthrough change efforts in the past? Can you leverage them for this initiative?

6. Develop a list of where in your network you can pull from if needed to fill specific gaps. Start listing specific names and qualifications of people you can call.

7. Develop your compelling proposition and recruiting speech for attracting the talented people that everyone else is also looking for. Why should they come to work with you on this breakthrough transformation?

8. Hold a kickoff meeting for the broader team that has now been assembled. Ensure that everyone understands the goals of the change initiative, the timeline, metrics, what success looks like, and how people will be measured.

9. Develop rules of engagement so that team leaders know the limits of their authority and feel empowered to make decisions and achieve results—for which you will hold them accountable.

10. Continue to monitor team performance to ensure that the team is operating well. Review the discussion in Step Two about trust and team dynamics. Is anyone not working out who thus needs to leave the team? This must be an ongoing activity.

11. Start a specific, cross-indexed contact list of talented people you may not need now but want to cultivate for future opportunities.

12. Develop long-term relationships with recruiters who are well suited to recruit in your arena, who have few conflicts that would keep them from tapping pools of talent, and who can get to know you personally so they can assess who fits with your style and also attractively describe you to potential hires.

9

Step Nine: Testing with Pilots to Increase Success

The premise underlying *Stacking the Deck* is that by building and effectively leading the right team, engaging in scrupulous advance planning, and undertaking a host of other tasks that have proven themselves to increase the odds of success, you and your team can foresee possible problems, work out solutions, and stack the deck in your favor. By carefully considering and executing each of the steps, you pave the way for success in implementing the breakthrough change you are championing. So the rest should be easy, right?

Not always. As each of the leaders you've heard from in this book can attest, breakthrough change continues to be challenging every single step of the way. The pilot and the rollout stages (which naturally overlap) are no exception, and we cannot overemphasize their importance.

Breakthrough change can manifest in many forms: a new product, a new process for doing things, a new technology platform, geographic expansion into new markets, even changes we haven't yet imagined. Defining a precise set of rules about how to roll out your next breakthrough initiative is impossible: the potential projects are simply too diverse. Nevertheless, appropriate and careful use of pilot projects is a consistent thread in successful rollouts; pilots can dramatically enhance your prospects for success. The focus of Step Nine is therefore on how to successfully employ pilot implementations.

A caveat before we begin: much as I strongly advocate using pilot projects, there are instances when it may seem you have no choice but to simply go forward with your change and forgo any testing.

Sometimes you have to balance the urgency of the need against the possible benefits of a pilot. For example, imagine if we had preceded our Internet trade pricing change at Schwab with a pilot in a select market. Lessons might well have emerged that would have helped with the full rollout. But we knew that customers were already upset at the pricing policy. There was just too much urgency and our pricing was too visible and transparent to the market for us to test the pricing change with different market geographies or customer segments.

This case, however, counts as an exception. More typically, there are plenty of opportunities to employ pilot implementations if you are creative. And as we'll see, there is no shortage of good reasons for using pilots.

PILOT PROJECTS ARE KEY

Pilots have historically been a big part of change initiatives. They provide ways to run small, select tests to determine if the change you're proposing is feasible and viable. Pilots can be run in different manners, different locations, different phases of the project, and for different purposes. Certain pilots are very specific to types of businesses. And some businesses are particularly adept at using them.

Starbucks is exceptional at making good use of pilots. In fact, they have a team dedicated to launching pilots around the world. As Howard Schultz explained, "We have people who manage and monitor our pilot tests, from proof of concept to scalability and everything in between. The ideas and concepts that aren't working fade away. The ones that are working get elevated to a larger number of stores over time. And if one is a big hit, it'll eventually be rolled out nationwide." This is core to their business, according to Schultz: "Our ability to scale a successful pilot to a bigger pilot, and then scale it nationwide or globally is the sweet spot of what we do."

To be clear, what we discuss here are not restricted to technology pilots or software beta tests. We focus on pilots that test significant changes to many aspects of a company's business model or production processes. If a company's training programs were shown to need major revisions and updating, a company might run pilot trainings for one module in different formats. Doing so would enable the company to get a head start on training and determine which of the formats—one-on-one training, in-class instruction, online instruction, or some combination—is the most efficient and cost-effective in transmitting the information and skills needed. The sections that follow provide information on traditional proof of concept pilots, scalability pilots, and in addition, one particular to the Stacking the Deck process.

Traditional Proof of Concept Pilot

If you have spent any amount of time in the business world, you've probably seen some version of a traditional proof of concept pilot implementation. These pilots rest on a belief that it makes the most sense to test a new idea on a representative sample of your customers and your employees. If you're a nationwide company in the United States, you want to launch a pilot in locations on both coasts, in the Southeast, Southwest, Midwest, and Rockies. You want to use some of your best managers, some middle-of-the-road managers, some high-performing locations, and some average ones. The goal here is to create a slice of life and then see how your idea performs in this micro but representative version of the real world.

This describes the most basic and traditional type of proof of concept pilot, and it's what Asurion's CEO Steve Ellis and I focused on when we began our discussion about the importance of pilot projects. We agreed that, as Steve said, "by creating a pilot, by showing people what's possible, you can short-circuit a lot of the negative, risk-averse reactions employees often have to breakthrough change." Steve explained that since big, breakthrough changes "create an amplifier effect on the issues that executives face in leading change, demonstrating to people what's possible can be enormously helpful."

How you structure this pilot and interpret the results can make or break a project over the long run. Unfortunately, when a traditional pilot to test the feasibility of a project shows initial success, leaders all too often rush to roll it out on a large scale. Because the entire team sponsoring the project has their reputations on the line, if the initial pilot results look promising then all too often a collective enthusiasm propels the project forward. For the same reason, if the data suggest weakness, it can be hard to scrutinize let alone walk away from the effort. The search for excuses often begins and another pilot test is mounted when the right action would be a very basic reconsideration of the change effort.

In addition, a proof of concept pilot is typically far removed from a test of scalability, the ability to take the change to the full breadth of the company's business. Since, as Steve estimates, 70 percent of big change efforts fail due to an inability to successfully scale the change, it's important not to shortchange the piloting phase or move too quickly. Unfortunately, by this time there is often so much pressure to bring the change to the marketplace on a large-scale basis that the critical step of properly executing the piloting process gets shortchanged.

Certainly traditional proof of concept pilots and scalability pilots are critical. But in my opinion these shouldn't be the first pilots undertaken. Instead, I advocate starting with a particular type of proof of concept as your initial test in the real world.

From Proof of Concept to Stacked Proof of Concept Pilots

The purpose of any pilot, particularly an early-stage proof of concept, is to see if the change you are proposing is even feasible. Will the desired effects transpire; will it produce the business advantage we are looking for?

There can be many ways to pilot test a concept. I recommend adding an even earlier, smaller pilot, which is designed in every way to succeed. I call this a *stacked proof of concept* pilot because it gives the advantages of stacking the deck to a proof of concept pilot. Its design is radically different in that it has been optimally configured to give your change, your idea, every possible opportunity to succeed. Instead of a wide range of geographical locations, you select the best possible location, where people (potential customers and staff alike) will be most receptive to the change you're proposing. Instead of addressing average customers, you target your ideal customer base, those segments most likely to respond positively. And instead of a cross section of managers and employees, you handpick your best and your brightest to work on the stacked proof of concept pilot. You're looking for those people who are drawn to and thrive on change. In fact, you want those "change junkies" who are actively excited about innovation, the people Steve Ellis referred to as the "five percent." Everyone you choose to be involved in the pilot team should be enthusiastic, forward-thinking, and completely on board with the change.

When you have thoroughly set up your stacked proof of concept pilot, your results are not projectable across the organization. If it fails, you are forced to concede that since your idea can't succeed here, it probably can't succeed *anywhere*, and needs to be fundamentally reconsidered. On the other hand, if the pilot is successful, you now have great advantages in attacking the next stage of the pilot process, as we'll discuss further on.

If an ordinary proof of concept pilot—one that's directed toward a typical cross section of your customer base and run by a typical cross section of your employees—fails, if your customers don't take to it or your management has trouble implementing it, it's natural to rationalize that failure. And rationalizations may come easily, in part because by the time you get to implementing the pilot step, you've already invested enormously in your breakthrough change initiative. You believe deeply in the urgent need for this change. You've spent time and energy on it and have devoted yourself to inspiring others to believe in the urgency and viability of this change. You have put yourself on the line with your superiors or the board to advocate for this change, stressing that it is something that needs to be done. It's no wonder you are primed to ignore and dismiss evidence that the initiative is flawed on a fundamental level. This is a very natural reaction, but not at all a helpful one.

After a failed pilot, you may find yourself focusing on the fact that there are many variables, many reasons an unoptimized pilot could fail outside of a fundamental flaw with the concept. When you conduct an ordinary proof of concept pilot and experience a failure, you wind up with a lot of potential questions to ask yourself, including:

- Was the incentive package we offered not sufficiently attractive?
- Was the training flawed? In what way?
- What did we overlook that we should have included?
- Did we not give the team enough money to implement the pilot successfully?
- Was the timeline too short?

But none of these questions and others that might come up after the fact really get at the meat of whether or not your change is fundamentally a good idea, one that can work. The tendency therefore is to modify some of the variables and go back to the market with another, similarly structured traditional proof of concept pilot.

Instead, starting with a stacked proof of concept pilot before undertaking a more typical proof of concept pilot allows you to guard against rationalizations. If you give yourself every chance to succeed and you still fail, you'll be forced to take a good, hard look at your original concept and honestly evaluate whether it is workable. In forming the pilot team and framing the project, you are trying to remove all possible implementation issues, individual motivation issues, employee push-back issues. All that is left is a single question: can this idea work? The stacked proof of concept pilot gives you the opportunity to test that question on its own and speaks to what Howard Schultz recommends when he says, "You want to fail fast . . . and write it off. Celebrate failures and mistakes not twice, but once. What can we learn and let's go!"

One criticism of an optimized, or stacked, proof of concept pilot is that by its very nature (using only the best and the brightest, throwing all available resources behind it) it doesn't provide information about how the idea performs in average or poor situations. That's certainly true; it's not a mirror of reality. But why not be better prepared before you take on reality? Why not gather as much information as you can before tackling a major change, so that you and your team can significantly increase your chances to succeed? That's what a stacked proof of concept pilot enables you to do.

Just be careful not to confuse a stacked proof of concept pilot with any other type of pilot, particularly not a scalability pilot. This approach is not a license to roll out the implementation company-wide. Instead it's a confirmation that your idea is viable, and it's a bit of preemptive insurance against big, public failure—a failure that could be incredibly difficult for the team or the company to bounce back from.

Of course, if you are lucky enough to have the resources, you may choose to test more than one stacked proof of concept pilot. Remember, the choices you make in stacking the pilot are your best guesses at what will be an optimal configuration. This may sound harder than it really is. Management typically knows where its best people, its strongest business conditions, and its situations most receptive to innovation can be found. But if you can conduct more than one stacked proof of concept pilot simultaneously, perhaps in different locations or focusing on different demographics, so much the better.

Naturally, the process doesn't end with a stacked proof of concept pilot or even a subsequent more traditional proof of concept pilot. Eventually, you will want to conduct a scalability pilot for viability on a large scale. Before turning to scalability pilots, we'll explore a few other points about testing.

Testing Before Transplanting a Concept

Even when a concept has worked elsewhere, it will need testing in a new environment. Variable pricing has been a staple in many industries and is particularly evident in the airline industry. As anyone who has compared prices with their seatmates on a flight knows, the price for a seat in the same section of a plane can vary widely, depending on an enormous number of factors, from date of purchase to date of travel and final destination. And that's not even factoring in any loyalty rewards.

Variable pricing hadn't yet come to the world of sporting events back when the San Francisco Giants were opening their new ballpark. As Larry Baer explained, one of his colleagues proposed instituting "what he called 'demand yield pricing.' He thought it would work, but wanted to test it. So we tried it for 2,000 or 3,000 seats a game.

The technology worked. The fans understood the concept that for the Dodgers or a bobblehead game they are going to pay a little more." After running this pilot test on a small scale, they continued to run pilots and eventually "rolled it out to the whole ballpark. It was a huge success and we estimated it could bring another $15 million annually to the bottom line." Larry's testing of this idea in high-demand Dodgers and bobblehead games was a version of a stacked proof of concept pilot.

The Giants' pilot of demand yield pricing allowed them to test a number of assumptions and determine answers. As it turned out, fans quickly adjusted to the changes in pricing and this system continues to help the team's bottom line. Plus, seats aren't empty and full stands make the Giants' ballpark a more exciting place to be.

Testing Assumptions, Minimizing Risks, and Gaining Advocates

Any sort of test is about validating or refuting assumptions. Therefore, before starting a pilot implementation of any sort, we should have a good sense of what assumptions we have, and thus the questions we need to ask. As just a few examples:

- We are assuming this change will make us more productive. Will it?
- We're assuming that customers will respond positively to this initiative. Will they?
- We are assuming that we can win over the employees. Can we?

A stacked proof of concept pilot can answer these questions and potentially force us to reevaluate our plan for implementing the change. For example, let's say we start our best managers in our best locations for the pilot. These highly skilled individuals know how to motivate and inspire their people, who in turn trust their leadership. So if we see people dragging their feet and resisting, we know that we have a problem. If these gold star managers can't get their people on board, then our average manager is really going to struggle—and may not get anywhere with the project. Because of this, we might reevaluate the amount of time we budget to get our employees behind the change. Maybe instead of two weeks of training and support we should plan for a month or even two or more. Or reconsider the entire implementation plan.

My failure to question my assumptions and test them with a pilot is why it took almost five years to get the branch network at Schwab to change toward a proactive client outreach culture that truly produced. In hindsight, it's clear that I wasted time—my own and everyone else's—because I tried to change a huge branch network all at once, working with many assumptions and few facts rather than testing my proposed changes, learning along the way, and building momentum.

It's true that pilots take time. But that time is insignificant when compared to the risks and damages that skipping over a proof of concept pilot can add.

Beyond testing assumptions, what else can a pilot offer? You want to know everything possible about how the implementation is working—or not—for your employees and your customers. It is often useful, after a pilot, to bring your managers together and ask them how they felt about the process:

- Did they feel that the training was adequate?
- What if anything did they learn from the process?
- Did they get frustrated? When? Why?
- Did the system actually work?
- How did the customers react?
- How did the employees react?
- What could we on the leadership team do better?

These questions and more are important to bring out in the open. Surprises are deadly when you are implementing breakthrough change; every question you answer is one less surprise down the road.

Additionally, the people who lead the pilot effort and come from the field can now advocate with their peers for this new idea. Once actual frontline employees are actively supporting the new idea, progress toward company-wide acceptance of a change can speed up.

An excellent example was the implementation of a new product line by our still relatively early-stage wealth management firm, High-Tower. When the company was about three years old, our CEO, Elliot Weissbluth, launched what he termed the HighTower lab, a place to test new ideas to bring to market. Two years later, the first product to make it through the lab's rigorous discussion process was brought to our board of directors. There was a significant amount of debate. "We are too early in our maturation to launch a new offering in the market. We don't have the management bandwidth and it will confuse the market as to what makes us unique," I suggested with an air of mature wisdom I enjoyed employing with our board from time to time.

Our trusting relationship created an atmosphere that supported spirited debate, and Elliot quickly disagreed, replying, "It's exactly what we need right now." He went on to describe the risk management he planned to employ along with his strategy to do two stacked proof of concept implementations staggered in time and in different markets. A healthy discussion ensued, and in the end we followed the carefully constructed plan of our CEO. He was ready for the board with a compelling vision of the future, a strong case for why the change was urgently needed, and how it tied to our mission.

The initiative also had some skeptics inside the broader employee ranks, people who sat in very influential positions. The stacked pilots were hugely successful; this won everyone over, and the offering moved forward with great success.

Often, by using multiple pilots either in sequence or in staggered stages, conducting separate pilots for different phases of the overall plan, you can speed up the entire rollout dramatically and begin seeing improvement in indicators early on. Another benefit of using multiple or staggered pilots is that just as you never get all the time and resources you want, you may rarely get enough money to roll out a big change all at once. If the overall change is going to happen in a series of steps anyway, it just makes sense to learn everything you can from each individual step.

From Proof of Concept to Scalability Pilots and Beyond

Of course, just as in any other strategy, wishful thinking can lead to an unsupportable reliance on pilots. Steve Ellis outlined the perils of putting too much emphasis on a proof of concept pilot: "Too often, people translate that very early success directly into execution mode before they're really ready for that. The definition of success in innovation or bold change is not simply proving whether the idea works or not—though that is important—it's about creating a scaled commercial implementation of that model, whatever it may be." Referred to as a scaled pilot or a scalability pilot, this step of testing the model on a broader scale is critical. Steve continued, "Where I most often see companies tripping up is in exactly this transition process. It's not enough to pilot purely for viability. Piloting for scalability is a big part of learning the barriers to change in your organization and figuring out how to get around them."

Steve's comments underscore one of the fundamentals of breakthrough change leadership: you must exploit every opportunity to increase the probability of success. One success does not guarantee another and even the greatest proof of concept pilot should not be relied on as definitive proof that a larger rollout will be destined to succeed.

As Steve says, "Too many people collapse right at the starting line in this process, because they've exerted all this organization energy and leadership attention and now we've got the model right. I've seen it time and time again: management declares that a pilot is successful and then no one wants to think through additional problems."

When I asked Steve about his own experiences with different varieties of pilots, I learned that he was actively involved with a series of pilots at the time of our interview. "We've recently done a pilot in Des Moines, Iowa, with a very, very creative way of delivering a point-of-need repair service and leveraging a domain name that we have. This pilot's been enormously successful, but it's only a proof of concept pilot. That's how we designed it, that's what we were looking for." He elaborated on the process: "Next week we have to go in and have a talk about where to go next, how we are going to expand our existing pilot to test whether this concept is truly scalable. We need to go from a concept that is laser-focused on this one specific market to something that we could spread across multiple markets without losing the basic root idea." Of course, that wouldn't be easy: "Since we have a service network of 30,000 field people, this is quite a large hurdle to get over. We are deliberately refusing to declare victory on the strength of this one pilot. Yes, now we know that the idea *can* work; next we need to see if it *will* work."

PILOTS DEMAND CONSTANT EVALUATION AND COORDINATION

This emphasis on the types of pilot tests that must be conducted and that are equally critical came up over and over in the interviews for *Stacking the Deck*. Unless you appreciate the differences, you run the risk of doing one without the other. Or overvaluing one over the other. Or simply not running enough pilots for thorough testing. As Dick Kovacevich told me, "The reason many projects are not achieved is that the leaders involved quickly convinced themselves that the project was achievable and then said, 'Okay. Let's roll this thing out.' But if the execution is flawed, suddenly you've got 80 percent of your people saying the project doesn't make sense anymore. Then you've got to go back and convince everyone that the project concept was fine; we just jumped the gun on large-scale implementation."

No matter how convincing your stacked proof of concept pilot may have been, you must also carefully implement traditional proof of concept and scalability pilots. You must think about a representative sampling of your average locations or management teams or customer segments well before rolling the project out full scale. Be sure to take the time to test your idea in the crucible of unresponsive customers, resistant employees, and less receptive locations. A stacked proof of concept pilot requires you to nurture your idea and give it every shot at success; a scalability pilot requires you to test and prepare for the implementation challenges that lie ahead. As Steve Ellis said, "We know that the idea *can* work"; now we must find the way to make it work in situations that are less than ideal if not outright challenging.

If I had known about the different types of pilots and their usefulness in a variety of situations when I was starting out in my career, I would have saved myself untold amounts of time and effort. One of the greatest benefits of pilots—and the multiple pilot systems—is that they enable us to discover problems and develop solutions while the scale is still limited and more manageable. This is important since there are always some things we can't fully understand until we do them. There are always problems that can't be foreseen; new challenges we didn't expect.

LOOKING TO THE FUTURE

As we look ahead to where a huge amount of innovation will come from, it's impossible to ignore the tidal wave of the human–technology interaction, which we are still trying to imagine, plan for, build, and exploit. Renée James's strong background in research and development has allowed her to stay ahead of this process at Intel: "I've always had a path-finding group working on a three-to-five-year view, in terms of R&D. We ask them to build the things that they are envisioning years out, using whatever technology we have today. Much of the time, you can create a working mock-up of the future with today's tools."

We wound up in a discussion about researching for the future—starting, even leaping toward it; testing what new technology may bring; even knowing that the necessary technology hasn't yet been developed. Instead, we explore the ideas and test to see where the greatest benefits may be, all while anticipating that when we've developed a clear strategy the technology will not be far behind. While the progress today in hardware is impressive, the progress in software-based services and solutions is especially noteworthy. The world of apps, the world of mobility and connectivity, is moving at light speed and is likely to transform business processes and whole industries. One of today's hottest topics is the "internet of things," referring to a new technology-enabled world with all kinds of new services, conveniences, and capabilities.

How does this world intersect with pilot implementations? If you're working in research and development at a high-tech company, you will sometimes create the front end of a project so that the consumer interaction looks smooth, polished, and fast enough to be computer-run, when in fact the back end is being handled manually. Effectively, this is a pilot of a pilot, enabling you to test the worth of an idea, the kernel of an innovation, and the various avenues of the process very early. It helps you see and explore the consumers' reactions, what they like and what they don't like. It lets you discover whether the idea resonates in the market before you expend the time and money perfecting the software, and long before you attempt to run the project to scale. Running a project in this way enables you to get ahead of where the world is (in this particular respect) and explore possibilities. It allows you to test the validity of an idea and learn, via experience, what details and processes will ultimately need to be built into the technology. We sometimes call this type of smooth front end with a simulated-technology back end (that is really a bunch of people running around to make something appear to be automated) "sneakerware," for obvious reasons. It's a good way of testing ideas before all the money is spent building something that doesn't win over consumers or employees in its early testing.

———

Pilots can be used in a variety of ways and combinations. They let you perfect the nuts and bolts of the process for your breakthrough change and dramatically increase the likelihood of its overall success. If you've prepared carefully and a pilot falls flat—if there's a fundamental flaw in the project—take the opportunity to learn and pivot. Know that the information you glean from a pilot is never wasted; instead, a failed pilot is a lesson, one that has averted the potential disaster of a failed project.

Use pilots early and often to unearth any problems with your change initiative and to develop necessary revisions. As you partition your project, you may find that phases and segments of the plan can be tested with pilots or multiple staggered pilots, maybe even with sneakerware. Test your assumptions, test the market, test your concept thoroughly before you even consider taking it to full scale—and use a scalability pilot before going to full rollout.

After investing time and energy preparing to bring about a break-through change, some leaders make the mistake of looking at the pilot step as a kind of gateway and believing that a successful pilot marks a clear passage to full implementation. This is flawed thinking. A pilot is a chance to acquire valuable information not typically available in any other way. It is a gift that helps you and your team be well prepared as you move toward the future you envision.

Once you and your team are confident that your breakthrough change is ready to be introduced or rolled out to the real world, you need to very carefully consider how you will do this. Even the most well-conceived and well-constructed changes need meticulous atten-tion through the rollout and beyond. We'll investigate this further in Chapter Ten.

STEP NINE ACTION ITEMS
TESTING WITH PILOTS TO INCREASE SUCCESS

1. Develop your basic piloting strategy. Can you carve out enough time to do several rounds of pilots? If yes, start by planning for a stacked proof of concept pilot to be followed by a traditional proof of concept (PoC) pilot, and after that a scalability pilot.

2. For your stacked PoC pilot, determine what your ideal target audience looks like (demographics, income, and so on).

3. Who in the company (for example, which store managers within given markets) are the best managers to lead the stacked PoC pilot?

4. How big should the stacked PoC pilot be and how long should it run?

5. What is the definition of success for the stacked PoC pilot, before moving to other pilots?

6. Run the stacked PoC pilot and document what worked and what did not work. Was it sufficiently successful to validate the basic idea?

7. If the pilot from item 6 was successful, identify whether any changes need to be made prior to rolling out a broader PoC pilot and well before moving on to the scalability pilot.

8. Design and execute a broader PoC pilot. Have the stacked PoC pilot field leaders help generate enthusiasm for the new pilot and the planned change effort. Evaluate the results. If positive, identify whether any changes must be made prior to the scalability pilot.

9. Design your scalability pilot. Create different situations to test the scalability of your idea (geographies, demographics, managers, and so on).

10. Execute the scalability pilot with an eye toward understanding what the rollout issues are with scaling this implementation to broad parts of the organization. Expect surprises and learning opportunities.

11. Develop metrics you can use to monitor the progress and success of the scalability pilots.

12. Evaluate the results of the scalability pilot and make necessary changes to the plan to implement the breakthrough change across the entire organization.

13. Build on what you learned from the scalability pilot, make the necessary changes, and roll out the change. Continue to stay on top of it since you still may learn that you need to fine-tune processes. Continue to communicate and lead.

PART TWO

LEADING THE CHANGE

Think of the steps described in Part One as footholds along the path leading to successful breakthrough change. But every path is different, each change has its own challenges, and all too often people and resources are stretched thin. The chapters of Part Two focus on the bigger picture, the leadership skills and mind-set you will need to drive change and maintain momentum for the long haul. Chapter Ten presents recommendations for sequencing the steps as you develop and implement breakthrough change. Chapter Eleven elaborates on the communication skills you will need throughout your initial change effort, and all successive ones. Chapter Twelve and the epilogue focus on innovation and the drive toward an unpredictable future for which you must prepare even as you begin to imagine it.

10

Using the Nine Steps to Bring Your Initiative to the Real World

Understanding each of the nine steps of the Stacking the Deck process provides a strong basis for leading breakthrough change. Now we need to examine how these steps fit together and build on each other. We'll then delve into additional topics to further prepare you to lead breakthrough change.

Stacking the Deck is written for an audience of emerging and more experienced executives, whatever your specific position. It is not intended as Management or Leadership 101; it does, however, emphasize critical aspects of those management and leadership skills that are especially necessary for success with initiatives of this nature.

NAVIGATING AND SEQUENCING THE NINE STEPS

Think how quick and easy change initiatives would be if you could simply move from one step to the next, each step getting you exactly one ninth of the way to the desired outcome. But the Stacking the Deck steps are neither literal nor linear. Instead you'll have to undertake some parts simultaneously; and occasionally you'll need to double back, to redo a previous step on the basis of the work in a subsequent step. These are not the directly linked steps of an escalator, nor are they as convoluted as the never-ending staircases depicted by the Dutch graphic artist M. C. Escher. They are, however, somewhat fluid in ways that can work to your advantage—now that you're alert to the process.

Step One, Establishing the Need to Change and a Sense of Urgency, is indeed the starting point for a breakthrough change initiative. But in most cases, the process of communicating the change extends to a very limited audience in the beginning. Since we don't yet have a team committed to the solution and we don't have a detailed or precise vision of what the solution is, we cannot go running around communicating that we have a problem. So with the proviso that Steps One, Two (Assembling and Unifying Your Leadership Team), and Three (Developing and Communicating a Clear and Compelling Vision of the Future) involve a small circle of executives, these steps can be considered as fairly linear.

In Step Four, Planning Ahead for Known and Unknown Barriers, we begin to expand the circle of active participants and bring more voices, players, and perspectives into the process. In doing so, we revisit Step One and communicate the need for change along with the vision of the future that we developed in Step Three. Our work on the barriers described in Step Four, particularly the section on planning for the unexpected, leads us into the planning process of Step Five.

Steps Five (Creating a Workable Plan), Six (Partitioning the Project and Building Momentum with Early Wins), and Seven (Defining Metrics, Developing Analytics, and Communicating Results) build on each other and connect to support transformative change. Aspects of these steps will need to be repeated and revised over time and the process remains incomplete until all points have been laid out and thoroughly enumerated.

Step Eight, Assessing, Recruiting, and Empowering the Broader Team, which will be hands-on throughout the initiative, will actually begin during Step Four, when the leadership team contemplates the potential barriers to overcome and the required skills. Looking ahead to determine the skills and experiences you will need is critical—since you may have to go outside the company to recruit if they don't exist within the company's existing pool of talent. Since this could consume considerable amounts of time, money, and effort, getting an early handle on your needs and working in parallel with the other steps is very important.

Step Nine, Testing with Pilots to Increase Success, is typically the last step to implement. But there can be exceptions. There may be instances in which a small pilot having a hand-picked team, a favorable market, and a minimally viable prototype can be tested very early in the life of the project.

The nine steps usually begin in the order presented in this book; the sequencing and overlap of steps will vary depending on circumstances. Figure 10.1 illustrates how the steps might be sequenced relative to each other. Precise timing will depend on circumstances and resources. Remember that there will naturally be some amount of overlap among steps and parallel work efforts along the way. After all, if breakthrough change were a straightforward, lockstep process, experienced leaders wouldn't constantly emphasize how difficult it is.

LEADING WITH CONVICTION

When Asurion's Steve Ellis and I were discussing the challenges of leadership and the difficulties in leading breakthrough change, he shared some thoughts that are especially relevant as you begin navigating the Stacking the Deck steps: "If you don't have true, deep, enduring conviction about the importance of the change you're pursuing, you will be buffeted, worn down, ground down, and diverted at those critical points where leadership is the only force that keeps the change moving. The biggest mistakes that I see come during those points. At root, the mistakes arise from the dissipation of conviction—leadership and management conviction."

Steve explains how the momentum at the start of an initiative can occasionally stall, leaving leaders in a tough spot: "There's always a lot of fanfare at the beginning of any big change. At this point, leaders can convince themselves that the change is important and needs to be treated with the appropriate urgency and energy. There's enormous energy put into the front end—in defining the point of arrival, establishing the management and communication infrastructure, creating the case for change, and assigning clear leadership and accountability. But all too often, people fail to fully appreciate what defines the finish line or the major milestones."

Step One
Establishing the Need to Change

Step Two
Assembling and Unifying Your Leadership Team

Step Three
Developing and Communicating a Clear and Compelling Vision of the Future

Step Four
Planning for Barriers Known and Unknown

Step Five
Creating a Workable Plan

Step Six
Partitioning the Project and Building Momentum with Early Wins

Step Seven
Defining Metrics, Developing Analytics, and Communicating Results

Step Eight
Assessing, Recruiting, and Empowering the Broader Team

Step Nine
Testing with Pilots to Increase Success

KEY:

Early thinking and preliminary action

Active leadership involvement

Ongoing activity with the broader team

Figure 10.1 Sequencing the Nine Steps

His thoughts reminded me of a hard lesson many CEOs learn while working with their boards: It is far easier and more productive to discuss weaknesses and strengths of the project at the outset rather than once it's under way. If you don't carefully consider the terms and resource needs until you are farther down the road, or if you overcommit, then your request for more time or money may be seen as a sign that you are slipping or missing your commitments. It is much better to negotiate these needs up front. Similar lessons also apply for non-CEO leaders of breakthrough change.

Steve and I both understood that the actual milestones for the change are not simply financial objectives. And they might not show up in classic metrics such as average hold time, volume of subscribers, efficiency metrics, revenue in a new market, working capital requirements, or any of the typical measurements that you might use to define the success of a change program.

"Instead," Steve added, "the breakthrough change actually requires people on the front lines of the business, the customer service reps, the field people, the person on the manufacturing floor, the rep taking the sales order, the person developing the new technology platform, to be thinking fundamentally differently about the nature of their jobs. They need to be open to learning to do new things, using new tools and capabilities, breaking old rules, upgrading their skills, investing in their own capabilities and the organization's capabilities to do something fundamentally different."

We agreed that when a change process is widely distributed along the front lines, "leaders have to touch potentially thousands if not tens of thousands of people" in order to make that change happen. "The distance between the PowerPoint slides and the proclamations and the strategy documents and that frontline person fundamentally embracing and executing this idea, with reliability and consistency, is simply enormous. The change process is a long road and there are so many potholes, diversions, and off-ramps along the way that leaders often underestimate what it takes." Steve knows what he's talking about, having learned these lessons firsthand: "Most leaders—myself included—almost always underestimate what it takes to get to that point. We fail to accurately define what bold change really is and what it really demands." Much as we might hope for an easier path, "there's simply no silver bullet for getting human beings to change. It's a ton of really, really hard, roll-up-your-sleeves work to accelerate the bold change process and to make it stick over time. Even with the best possible strategies, you'll need the time, energy, and emotional fortitude to carry, pull, or drag the organization through those ebbs in conviction when people are seeing all the pain of the change and none of the benefit. That dip in morale is always a perilous point in any change process."

What Steve was saying resonated with me. I knew how critical it was to get past the dips Steve was describing when he said, "The longer this kind of dip goes on, the more the change will dissipate and diffuse. You'll never even get to the point that people in the front lines have fundamentally changed the way they do things—or see that outcome you were looking for when you proposed your change." As he said, "If you're not ready to carry on through those moments and you haven't personally built up your reserves and anticipated the need for a sustained investment of resources, financials, human capital, and emotional endurance, then you will not survive those trying moments."

Sobering words, but important thoughts for leaders at all levels to bear in mind. Whether in the boardroom or managing operations on the ground, leaders need the conviction, the determination, and the energy to see the change through.

NEGOTIATING TERMS

The CEO needs first to negotiate with the board regarding expectations for a breakthrough change initiative. But what of the operator who will be tasked with *actually leading the change* on the ground? Imagine a major initiative that might just transform the future of your organization. Your superiors have already navigated Steps One and Three and they are looking to fill out the leadership team, complete Step Two, and get the project rolling. The project involves a certain level of risk, and to mitigate that vulnerability they need a strong, capable leader to organize the initiative. Then your boss walks in to inform you that you have been selected to lead this critical, but risky initiative. What do you do?

You may well be eager to launch your project and get a sense of exactly what it requires, while shoring up your own bargaining position with some incremental successes. But starting too quickly may be a mistake. You have the most leverage *before* the project begins—perhaps even before you formally sign on. So before you irrevocably accept this assignment and get rolling, you need to thoughtfully assess the resources you have been assigned and establish clear parameters of success and failure for your efforts. The board may have seen the big picture, but you need to carefully consider Steps Two, Three, Four, and Five as you begin the process of negotiation. Resources, deadlines, deliverables, and decision rights are the major terms you need to codify and agree upon early in the process.

It's tempting to think that success and failure are clear, distinct, and self-evident. A project that invests $5 million and makes $12 million is a success, right? But what if it was supposed to make $20 million? The difference between success and failure can be completely in the eye of the beholder. How we set and negotiate expectations with our superiors or with shareholders and analysts can determine whether a breakthrough change is hailed as a huge success or seen as long overdue or, much worse, too little too late.

You want to lead this project, but as you hear about the thinking that's already begun to develop, your sense is that the expected outcomes are entirely too aggressive. They want too much, too fast, and with too few of the resources you believe are necessary. This is nothing new in business. Leadership is all about setting high expectations and then inspiring the team to strive toward success. You can't simply communicate deadlines and deliverables upward; instead, you need to negotiate from a place of strength and knowledge to secure the best possible framework for your project.

Be aware that you may be setting yourself up for difficulty and disappointment if you agree to take on the project as is. When you (inevitably) disappoint sky-high expectations, it is seen as your fault rather than the result of overly ambitious initial terms. There is typically little room for renegotiating terms after the fact or explaining away the reasons for a failure that "wasn't your fault."

The time to set the terms then is at the outset of the initiative. You must also be very clear with your team members about where *their* responsibilities and duties begin and end. Just as you have to carve out your own authority, you must do so for the people under you. Don't postpone these conversations.

You may not be able to get everything you want or need in the beginning. There are some firm limits in any negotiations. But a thorough conversation early on can help you discover where there is give. The deadline may be dictated by the realities of competition or already negotiated and set at a higher level of the organization. But perhaps the deliverable can be scaled back to a pilot implementation or a limited-scale rollout that will require less time and money than a full implementation.

Decision rights, unlike deadlines and resources, are more flexible and perhaps the most dependent on early negotiation. You need to know what decisions you are allowed to make, how fast you can move, and when exactly you need to get higher-level approvals. If you establish yourself as someone willing to accept an extraordinary amount of managerial oversight without argument, or wait until your project is already under way to begin asserting yourself, you will find it very difficult to get away from that initial perception.

You will be held responsible for the initiative's outcome, as well you should be. You must therefore negotiate carefully up front, nailing down as many issues as possible and with as much precision as possible. Understand that when you take on a breakthrough effort, you take on responsibility for any development and may be held accountable for decisions you neither made nor recommended. Sometimes that's exactly what must happen. Keep the big picture in mind and control what you can.

GETTING STARTED

Whether you are the CEO or the operator driving the breakthrough change, bear in mind that—as a Schwab colleague pointed out to me years ago—it's important to "go slow to go fast." Greater diligence in the early planning stages of a project may allow multiple teams to work simultaneously on multiple threads and achieve a significant effort for less money and in a shorter amount of time. For those of us who are eager to get going, who can't wait for the future, this can be a difficult concept to embrace.

This has never been easy for me since I am typically mired in the idea of "go fast and then go faster"—at least until some particularly strong form of resistance pops up to remind me. Try as I might to change it, my instinct is never to "go slow to go fast." This shortcoming is but one example of how diversity on the leadership team can pay off. I have surrounded myself with people who fully understand the importance of going slowly and carefully at the outset and who know to push back when my own instincts for speed are getting in the way. This is one of many skills I am still working on. Whatever yours are, be sure you've included people whose strengths counterbalance your weaknesses.

Once the leadership team is on board at the beginning of big, breakthrough change initiatives, many (if not most) of these leaders will want to get rolling and begin to see "real" progress. And by "real" progress they often mean seeing change actually happening, not just a bunch of people conducting endless meetings mapping out a transformational breakthrough effort. Still, these slow, methodical steps are exactly what is needed and anything else will result in disappointment and wasted time, effort, and money.

In addition to the reminders to go slow to go fast, the principles described in Geoffrey Moore's classic, *Crossing the Chasm*, can provide immensely helpful information. Often, especially in the high-tech world, you can find an audience who will adopt almost any new idea. These "early adopters," as Moore refers to them, will overcome bugs, inconveniences, poor service, inadequate user manuals, and other difficulties in order to have the latest technology. They buy in to new product concepts early, not for the novelty or to be first, but because they can "imagine, understand, and appreciate the benefits." In retrospect, this idea made clear why a number of programs we developed early on at Schwab took off with a certain group of investors and then stopped growing. For example, we developed personal accounting software called "Financial Independence," which had a solid if not spectacular launch. We had satisfied Moore's "early adopters"; however, we did not have the organizational structure and operating discipline to improve the programs fast enough to reach a larger market. With a faster cycle time, we might have been able to learn what wasn't working for consumers and then change the programs to appeal also to Moore's "early majority," the roughly one third of potential customers who simply won't tolerate the glitches or problems that early adopters accept.

Having not succeeded with this middle group, we didn't stand a chance of attracting the "late majority" (the final third) who watch and wait, not buying until the product or program "has become an established standard." Our success with the early adopters simply could not translate to a larger group because we had not crossed the chasm Moore describes. In contrast, Scott Cook and Tom Proulx had enormous success in creating and constantly improving Intuit's Quicken, personal finance software that was easy to use, intuitive, and ever evolving.

In many ways, the ideas Moore presents parallel the ideas behind proof of concept versus scalability pilots. Just because something works once or works with a select group does not mean it is ready for widespread rollout and the harsh test of mainstream reality. In fact, as Moore's book title telegraphs, there are chasms between groups; it's crossing those chasms that presents the challenges. Whether our initial success comes from a pilot or a rollout to the early adopters, ultimate success depends on building momentum and recognizing that early, initial success is just that. It's the beginning of bringing the initiative out to the world, not the end.

DEALING WITH THE RISK OF FAILURE

When we talk about breakthrough change and pioneers, we must inevitably talk about the risk of failure—perhaps even on a large scale. Your people are going to be nervous about the prospect of risking their careers and reputations on untested ideas. What then should a leader say when asked, "What are the personal consequences if we are not successful here? Is it okay to fail?"

These are difficult questions. Leaders certainly can't say, "Sure, it's perfectly okay to fail!" because it's usually not. An answer that is often heard is, "Well, it depends." Obviously, this is more of a non-answer and doesn't offer any useful or reassuring guidance.

Noble Failures Balance the Risk

In an attempt to better answer these often unstated questions about failure, I have elaborated on a concept called Noble Failure. I knew that, as the Irish poet, critic, and educator Edward Dowden (1843–1913) put it, "Sometimes a noble failure serves the world as faithfully as a distinguished success." But I suspected that these words from his time would not allay people's fears today. For example, who decides if my failure is "noble"?

I have contemplated the concept of Noble Failure and given it specific conditions. The concept reflects the recognition that big breakthrough change initiatives inevitably run the risk of failing. And it is an acknowledgment that often failure is not a result of incompetence or lack of effort; instead, it is due to any number of factors over which you have limited control. Projects can still fail even if you carefully go through every step in the Stacking the Deck process: stacking the deck cannot guarantee success. Perhaps the idea behind your initiative was fundamentally flawed. Or perhaps as you were in the middle of the project, another company came out with a superior product. These are the kinds of risks that you can never fully avoid or neutralize. We need a new category of failure to describe such situations.

Noble Failure, in my view, has seven important conditions:

1. The project was *well planned.* You did your homework and you crunched the numbers. You used intuition where appropriate.
2. You *failed smart and small.* Whenever possible, you confined your failure to the lab or a pilot program like those covered in Chapter Nine. You used models and prototypes and conducted lower-cost tests whenever feasible.

3. You had a *contingency plan*. You knew the places where the plan was most likely to get off track and were prepared to slow it down and steer carefully through the curves if necessary.
4. You *didn't bet the company*. The failure didn't cost so much money that the company is now in financial trouble. You considered opportunities to syndicate the risk with other organizations if appropriate.
5. You *limited the negative* fallout. This failure was not hugely public; it didn't cause a compliance, legal, or public relations fiasco. You did not imperil the company's reputation.
6. You followed a policy of *"no surprises"* with your superiors. If the project was struggling, you let management know so they could potentially help you or prepare contingency plans you had not thought of.
7. You *learned from your experience*. After a Noble Failure, you conducted a postmortem and tried to extract learning opportunities from this experience both for yourself and for the organization.

If each of these conditions has been considered and observed in depth, before, during, and after the effort, then the outcome may be thought of as a Noble Failure. In that case, what we don't do is punish the person or the team who originally proposed, advocated, or led the change. This is not about rewarding failure but rather about not punishing courage and innovation. Ideally, with the company culture behind you, a Noble Failure is a kind of neutral for your career: you don't advance, but you do survive professionally. It may even be a benefit, because you now have the experience of trying and failing and can apply that experience and the lessons you've learned to future projects. The Noble Failure concept is intended to encourage people to voice their opinions and ideas more freely because they know that even a failing effort will be tolerated, sometimes even celebrated, and never punished.

Early in my Schwab days, we developed online trading software called the "Equalizer" (sadly, I am responsible for that corny name). Because no other discount trading firm had such a product, it garnered a small, very loyal following. It just wasn't user-friendly enough to attract a big and profitable client base. We learned from this experiment and years later replaced it with "StreetSmart" software based on an early version of Windows (and better named by someone else). This was much more successful, but it certainly wasn't a breakthrough. However, no one's career suffered for the lack of breakthrough success with either of these software products. Instead these efforts prepared us for the Internet and the explosion of online trading that followed. Because of these efforts, we all learned what we needed to set ourselves up for success in online trading. This was Noble Failure at its best and ultimately led to StreetSmart Edge® and StreetSmart Pro®, vastly reengineered products which are part of Schwab's services today.

Anticipate and Manage the Risks

It is true that breakthrough change takes even longer if things go wrong. The planning processes included in Steps Four, Five, and Six are the best, most efficient time to take a preventative look at risk factors and develop strategies to mitigate them. The process of assessing and planning for risks is not something you do once and you are done. It is a constant activity, since conditions change and new risks can come at any time from a host of places. For instance, scope creep (below) never goes away. It remains a risk right to the conclusion of the initiative.

Risk factors can develop from both from inside and outside the company. Anticipating and managing through internal risk factors is much more straightforward than dealing with the external kind, such as regulatory changes or strategic moves by competitors, which can drop roadblocks in your path. These obstacles are generally hard to anticipate, so you must be forever vigilant looking for early indications that adversity is lurking on the horizon. The sheer number of outside complications that might influence your organization means that it's impossible to develop enough Plan Bs to counter every vulnerability.

As much as you try to identify and plan to deal with risk, there will always be uncertainty when you are breaking new ground—and you must learn to live with that uncertainty. Indeed, your ability to lead and inspire in the face of uncertainty is an important part of the breakthrough change process. If you've worked through the Stacking the Deck steps, you should already have identified some areas of risk. Over the course of my career, I have managed to sort the risk factors of breakthrough change into seven planning categories. Developing an awareness and a plan for these problems won't save you if something in the market goes awry or a competitor scoops you, but it will allow you to protect your project structure from those hindrances that you can manage or even avoid.

Scope Creep   From the outside, adding new elements to a breakthrough change initiative might seem productive and logical. Since we are already changing so much, why not add a few more things to the list? You will have to stand firm on the boundaries of the change and resist suggestions that might overwhelm the focus of the project. This will not be easy. Some of the impetus for scope creep may come from your own team, or even from the face in the mirror. Resist! Put these new ideas into Phase Two or Release 2.0 of your initiative.

The Technological Stretch   You have to contextualize this risk in more than one way. Essentially, you want to take this query through three descending levels:

- Has this technological change ever been done?
- Has it ever been done in our industry?
- Has it ever been done in our organization?

As you can imagine, the risk decreases steadily as you get closer and closer to your organization. The more commonly utilized a technology is, the easier it will be to find the talent and experience you will need to be successful. If your idea is something that has been done in the industry, then you might already have reliable consultants to bring onto your team. Even better, if something similar has been done in your organization before, you may be able to readily access the expertise you need within your own organization via a reassignment or loan. But if the change you are proposing involves something that has never or rarely been done before, anywhere, you are taking on a much larger risk. Sometimes you have to evaluate whether the "bleeding edge" is worth the potential risk. This is a very tough call. After all, it's called the bleeding edge for good reason.

Consider the Apple Newton. Released in 1993, it relied on handwriting recognition, a risk that turned into a bad gamble because the feature fell far short of expectations, hurting Apple. The early digital assistant insight was essentially on point, but the way it became expressed and executed was a failure, particularly once Blackberry broadly commercialized the breakthrough innovation of tiny handheld keyboards and thumb typing. In time, the Newton concept of the touchscreen became a major driver in mobile technology innovations, including Apple's iPhone and iPad.

The Business Stretch   This is the flip side of familiarity with the technology focus. As such, the questions are quite similar:

- Has a project like this ever been done?
- Has it ever been done in our industry?
- Has it ever been done in our organization?

You need to know if the company has ever done anything similar from a business model or conceptual design perspective. Is what you are proposing totally foreign to the people within your organization? What about the managerial structure? What about cultural implications?

In suggesting that we change how the Schwab branch offices interacted with customers, I failed to realize how novel the change would be to Schwab. The change was nothing new within the traditional brokerage industry, but it was totally new to Schwab. It seemed like a small issue, but it actually required employees to essentially do the opposite of what they had always done: be proactive rather than reactive. A change that is foreign to the company can work, but it's going to take longer and cost far more, and it will need to generate sufficient benefits to be worth the effort.

Maintaining the Team Through the Project   Once you have developed a strong team for your project, you need a strategy to maintain them as a group and as individual contributors. Breakthrough change initiatives are very challenging, especially for the members of the core team. The excitement and momentum that you have carefully built can evaporate as an initiative stretches into months and years. Difficulties, coupled with a protracted time frame, can put a lot of stress on team members; over time, all this can reduce their morale. Success, on the other hand, can be something of a double-edged sword. The higher profile your project, and the more outstanding the results, the greater the likelihood that team members will be recruited for other opportunities both inside and outside the company.

Be prepared for long-duration projects to test your resolve and the resolve of everyone around you. Be sure to put in time and effort to keep team morale high. The time required to do so is substantial—and absolutely necessary. Breakthrough change is a lengthy process. You can reduce the impression of the project taking too long and maintain momentum by breaking the effort down into smaller components early on, as described in Chapter Six.

Keeping Management on Board   Your superiors will likely not be comfortable with a change that plays out without interim results over an extended time, and competitors are certainly not sitting around and waiting. The best way to prevent a loss of interest and resolve is to make sure that you keep management in the loop at all times. Just as you need to build and maintain excitement about the project among your team members, you need to do so at every other level of the organization. This includes your shareholders, investors, suppliers, customers, and bosses, as well as your subordinates. You have to get them on board, build excitement about the project and its progress, and keep them looking forward. As you do this, realize that the stakes go up. The higher the project's visibility, the more important success becomes to the organization—and to you.

Investment Size   You need to be honest about the size of this change. Risk increases proportionately with size. Is this a $2 million change or a $20 million change? Of course, financial size is a relative matter. To some organizations a $5 million project is a rounding error, and to others it is a bet-the-company investment. You must determine what kind of impact a failure would have on the organization as a whole. Is this a bet-the-company change? Or is it, potentially, a storm the company could weather? This is not to say that you shouldn't initiate bet-the-company changes—I've done it myself—but you may have to reconcile yourself to significant personal risk, as well as risk to the organization as a whole. It is my very personal belief that you don't financially bet the company unless competitive circumstances demand such a move and everyone in leadership is totally behind you.

Quality of the Planning Effort   If you have followed all the steps up to this point, you will have already mitigated this potential problem. Remember that too much optimism can have a detrimental effect on your ability to plan. But you can also sabotage your plans if you are unable to recognize potential problems and create contingency plans. As discussed in Chapter Seven, clear and consistent metrics that let you know the limitations and see the warning signs are critical. If you skimp on the legwork at the beginning, you may be blindsided by one or more of these risk factors later on.

Even if you carefully and diligently follow the nine-step process, negotiate terms, and consider the various issues and risks, you cannot guarantee success. Bringing initiatives to the real world is fraught with challenges. Given the history of breakthrough change initiatives, you already know the deck is almost always stacked against you. To give yourself the best chance of succeeding you must combine a tested, thoughtful process with an extraordinary dose of leadership. Bookstore shelves are packed with wonderful books on leadership. I encourage you to explore them all, to read the classic ones, and to stay current on the new ones.

Bold, breakthrough change requires leaders at all levels who can demonstrate courage and inspiration. This is seen in how they communicate with their teams. Unfortunately, solid communication skills are quite rare—and are therefore the topic of the next chapter.

11

Communicating and Connecting to Inspire

At its most fundamental level, leadership depends on the ability to communicate effectively and in ways that inspire people to action. Leadership communication skills are integral to every step of the Stacking the Deck process. This chapter focuses on the topics of communication and character, illustrating their connection to inspiring action and successfully leading breakthrough change.

Citi's Debby Hopkins emphasized the importance of communication. From her perspective, "to succeed, leaders must bring people along. You must let people voice their concerns, and even voice their dissent. Sometimes you may think to yourself, 'Are you kidding? I've answered that question 42 times!' But I suggest you step back, take a breath, and fashion a simple and clear core message that people will take away—and remember."

If character and genuine connection don't come across in leaders' communications, frequency alone will not engender inspiration. Often the effort required to communicate and connect is difficult and time consuming, even while time may be at a premium. Ginger Graham, CEO of Two Trees Consulting, put some of the challenges front and center. "The change process requires a tremendous amount of communication. However, as they are developing the plan, executives spend time behind closed doors, planning and budgeting. They have secret meetings to consider workforce reductions and who may be involved. They hide from employees, in part because they don't want to be asked any questions they can't yet answer."

If executives are not putting themselves in situations that showcase their character, how can would-be followers determine if these leaders deserve to be followed? Ultimately, the willingness to follow stems from observing how leaders communicate and connect, how they demonstrate their character, and how they make the changes they are advocating real to their constituents.

LEADERSHIP COMMUNICATION MUST BE AUTHENTIC

Leading breakthrough change will test every aspect of your leadership abilities; your communication skills are certainly no exception. If you don't have the tools to speak effectively to people, how can you possibly inspire their passion or convince them of the necessity for the change?

There is far more to being an effective communicator than most executives believe—at least when they are starting out. During the first 20 years of my career I thought I was pretty good at speaking to my teams and motivating them. In reality, I was barely scratching the surface on the skills I would need to lead the change initiatives that were waiting for me. After I had been with Schwab for about eight years, my boss Larry Stupski had a near fatal heart attack. To everyone's surprise (including my own) I was promoted to fill his position as president and chief operating officer. Initially, I felt quite capable of handling this elevated assignment. After a few months, however, it was apparent I had assumed a whole new level of leadership responsibility for which I was not just underprepared, but unprepared.

As one of my remediation strategies, I went looking for a speechwriter to help me sharpen my communication within the company. When a colleague introduced me to Terry Pearce, a communication consultant and the founder and president of Leadership Communication, I thought I was getting a speechwriter. I had no idea what was really ahead.

For our first project together, I wanted some help with a speech I needed to give to the 200 top executives within our then

3,500-person company. I'd never worked intensively with a speech-writer and wasn't sure what to expect. Whatever vague notions I did have were soon blown out of the water.

As I finished telling Terry what I wanted him to do, he interrupted me. "I can do that, Dave, but I don't think what you have in mind is really what you want to say." Truthfully, I was taken aback. He went on. "If we really want to inspire these people, I need you to spend some time talking to me about who you are and what experiences have shaped your life. I need to know what moves you, what your values are, what motivates you when you have won and when you have lost. I need to know who you are and why you care about all of this as passionately as you do. Then we can work on this speech you have coming up."

I was flabbergasted. I wasn't looking for someone to help me write an autobiography. I wanted a damn speech! My response was immediate. "Terry, I'm a really busy guy. This seems like a lot of busywork for a speech. Can't we just discuss the message I want to deliver and then you find a really clear and compelling way for me to say it?" Frustration was entering my tone of voice.

"Sorry, Dave, that's not really what I do," was his reply. "There are lots of people who are good with words, and sometimes that works for articles, but that's not what we need right now. Everyone knows the topic because you have been working on this change for a while. It's less about *what* you say and more about *how* you say it and whether or not it is authentic. You need to deliver a message that will be compelling because everyone understands and believes your personal commitment to what you want them to do, and that you believe it is not only in *your* best interest, but in *their* best interest as well. Once they sign up for the values embedded in what you are suggesting, their actions will follow. Certainly the facts are important, but to inspire, you must be authentic and speak from the heart. After all, they are following you, not just the idea. Both are important—and this is what leadership communication is all about."

It was quickly apparent that I hadn't hired a speechwriter but a communication expert and a leadership coach. I was incredibly lucky to have stumbled into this relationship, which continued for the rest of my tenure at Schwab, and beyond. We recently worked together on a speech, and once again the collaboration was magic. We were dynamic partners, and at the peak of our work together at Schwab, we wrote *Clicks and Mortar*, a top-ten best seller on *BusinessWeek* and on Amazon; it was also a best seller in Germany.

Terry is also the author of a best-selling book on leadership communication called *Leading Out Loud*, currently in its third edition. I consider it the bible on this subject, and I assign it to all my students. Essentially all my ideas and all I know about this subject come from what I have learned from Terry's coaching and what I experienced while we were working together. When my leadership communication has been most genuine and most effective in inspiring people, it has been thanks to Terry's coaching and to his advice and reminders that have become part of me.

Make Values Visible

Howard Schultz reflected on exactly what Terry and I had so often discussed during our work together: facts are important yet it's values and authenticity that make the difference. Howard told me about guiding Starbucks through a very challenging time. His story is a perfect example of how effective, empathetic communication, a commitment to culture building, and the character of the leader can be a foundation for a breakthrough change project and then contribute to making that change a reality.

He began by explaining, "It was back in January of 2008, at the height of the cataclysmic financial crisis. Things weren't just bad—they were brutal. I created what I thought of as a kind of 'first 100 days.' I knew what I was going to do and how I was going to do it. What I didn't know was that things were even worse than I'd anticipated and continuing to nose-dive, mainly because of the economic issues." Howard had a clear idea of how customers viewed his product in this environment: "Starbucks products are, more than anything else, discretionary purchases. So it is our job to *create* demand, innovation, and desire."

By that point, he knew that "the cost structure of the company was not going to get us through the economic downturn." His first week back as chief executive officer, he gave a speech to the entire company; four thousand people viewed it in person and the rest via webcast. Howard explained, "The first thing I did was stand up and apologize. And I cried. I hadn't gone in there planning to cry, but I was apologizing that we as leaders had let them, the workers and their families, down." Schultz knew, however, that "we can't rewrite the past. We can only face the future, together. And I explained that we were going to have to make significant cuts and tough decisions to save the company."

Friends and colleagues had cautioned him to be careful with what he disclosed because the facts could scare people. "But," Howard said, "one of the first questions about leading bold change and being a leader is, do you tell the truth? Do you parse out information or do you trust your people? When you are asking people to follow you and believe in you, how could you give them anything but everything, in terms of information?" Howard decided "that every time I had information that was important for them to know, I gave it to them. Even if it was hard to hear or frightening."

Howard also had a clear idea of the one role that was crucial during this time. He understood that "the most important person in the history of the company is the store manager—and I needed a method to talk to every store manager. How could I get ten thousand people in one room?" It was not an easy proposition and bound to be expensive. Naturally, "the board had objections, because the cost would be well into the millions. I asked them: 'Where better to make an investment in the turnaround of this company? Where else than in our people?' We debated it, looked at alternatives, and in the end we all agreed that the situation and the opportunity to generate passion and commitment justified the expense."

As the conference began, in October 2008, Starbucks was "running negative 8 percent comps and our comparable sales statistics were getting worse every week and every month." Starbucks had never had negative comp store sales in its history. Howard "knew that when we got to negative 14.5 percent, we were going to run out of money—and we were heading for negative 20 percent. That knowledge was in my head as I prepared my speech for the last day of the conference."

Again friends and colleagues warned him that people would not be able to absorb the information. Howard explained, "Of course I worried about scaring people. But I also knew that if people didn't know just how bad the situation was, they weren't going to be able to understand what they had to do to manage and lead their stores. I decided on full transparency."

Howard focused his speech on two words: *bystander* and *accountable*. "I talked about what it means to be personally accountable for everything that goes on, everything that you see and hear. And I talked about what it means to not be a bystander. I told them, 'If we get to negative 14.5 percent, we are all going to be out of a job.' I was pleading for them to understand when I said, 'What if this was one store? You own the store. And the food on your table is dependent on what happened that day. That is what we have to do.' Because every single customer, every single transaction, every single interaction mattered more than ever before."

Howard well understands that his "speech alone did not make the company more profitable right away; but afterwards, it never got worse. It took over a year, but we did turn it around." His story is, to me, a great illustration of the power of genuine communication. And "genuine" is a key word here.

This book has emphasized that change is an emotional issue. In further elucidating his discussion of change, Terry Pearce explained that "change can seem chaotic, senseless, and frightening—and that is why people hate it. But progress is different. It is change with an underlying worthwhile challenge and purpose." We both understood that for people to see a change as progress, "the narrative of where we are going has to look better than the narrative of where we have been. It also has to look better than where we could wind up if we continue, without making the proposed change." We need the stories and retellings of personal experiences that are forward thinking, inspiring, and that appeal to our emotional foundations.

Engage with Stories

As a numbers guy, I needed a long time to fully appreciate that if you want to overcome emotional objections you cannot rely on facts and figures alone. It's a lesson I've had to relearn too many times. When I've forgotten it or discounted Terry's advice to "rely heavily on stories, experiences, metaphor, and image," my presentations have been relatively ineffective. Numbers may seem a faster way to make a point, but it's stories that people remember. While Howard mentioned a few financial facts about Starbucks' situation back in 2008, his speech mostly comprised stories about what had made the company successful and what needed to change to get it back on the path to future success. He talked about the managers and baristas in the stores who talked to customers every day, who welcomed them into the store and created the emotional connection with customers that makes Starbucks "the third place" in people's lives after their homes and their place of work.

The personal experiences and stories you share with others create the emotional engagement that begins the transformation of "change" into "progress." It's how you build the purpose behind the change that gives it meaning and allows for buy-in, not just practically but emotionally as well. Unfortunately, executives—even those with the experience to know better—all too often fall into the trap of giving employees reams of facts, statistics, and numbers to create the case for change. This may work with your board, but if you want to encourage those whose lives and daily activities will be directly affected by your change initiative, then stories are the way to begin overcoming emotional resistance and generating engagement.

This need for engagement came up over and over again in the interviews for this book, as well as my own experience. You can't simply demand the support of the people on the front lines who will be affected by your change initiative. You must earn it. And money can buy only a small portion of the support that you will need. Money doesn't inspire; it motivates. That gets you people's hands. It is *meaning* that gets their hearts, meaning that fuels people's discretionary effort, their thinking, action, and desire to be active members of the project team and their willingness to disrupt daily existence on the front lines to do things a new way. Communicating about change is less about *motivation* (the exchange of behaviors for rewards) and more about *inspiration* (appealing to an innate desire to be a part of and contribute to something really important). Hence inspirational communication is a must for leading breakthrough change.

A Gallup survey asked a group of executives to appraise themselves on whether or not they were inspirational communicators. Then their followers were asked whether these executives were inspirational. You may not be surprised to learn that there was something of a discrepancy in the results: executives thought that they were doing just fantastic, inspiring everyone. Of the executives, 93 percent said that they were "very or somewhat effective in inspiring communications." Unfortunately for them (and for their companies), only 26 percent of their followers rated them as inspirational communicators. Obviously, it is the opinion of the followers that matters here.

Top executives usually get where they are because they have a high aptitude for business and they are skilled in their areas of expertise, such as accounting, technology, marketing, and the like. They take responsibility for outcomes, they speak with clarity, and exhibit emotional control. They are expert at what they do, they are good at managing to drive results, and they get promoted up the ranks.

Less frequently do top executives (or members of boards of directors) achieve their career success on the basis of their ability to *emotionally connect* with people. You can go very far in corporate life with good technical skills, a clear voice, and the ability—and willingness—to hold yourself and others responsible and accountable. But the leadership skills required for breakthrough change demand more. These initiatives are long and difficult, and the road to success is often paved with setbacks and disappointments. To keep the team moving forward, leaders must connect with those they lead. This means they must be, and be seen as, trustworthy, empathetic, courageous, passionate, and resolute. Employees must admire you not just for your competence but also for your strength of character. You earn the loyalty of those around you by what you do, who you are, and how you talk about what is important to you.

The world is changing. I see that boards of directors, in discussing the relative characteristics of leadership candidates, often focus now on evidence of emotional intelligence and the ability to inspire others, as well as on competencies and other work experience. Perhaps we are all moving toward "and" solutions: leaders must continue to be concerned with outcomes and metrics; they must be competent in all the traditional senses—*and* they must be trustworthy, empathetic, and able to communicate in ways that inspire those around them. In looking at the impact of these principles, Terry and I determined that competence and connection are the key indicators of the most successful leaders. Competence alone has enabled many successful executive careers. But to become an authentic leader capable of guiding breakthrough change, we must be able to display our competence and connect with the people we hope to lead.

Competence and connection need to be evident. All too often, when we focus on how to communicate, we think of "good communicators" as people who have a certain kind of body language or who plan out their speeches in a specific way. We may be focusing on the wrong issues and aspects of leadership. Being an effective communicator demands much more than showing up at the podium on time and reading a speech without tripping over any lines. That would be easy compared to what's really needed.

Be Fully Present

When I was at Schwab, I had a very specific way of approaching all my speeches. Terry and I would work on what I needed to communicate and on the stories or anecdotes that would add power and authenticity to the speech. Terry would then write out the speech very precisely, word for word, as though I was going to use it as a script. Then I would read it aloud over and over. Eventually, I would boil it down to a few specific bullet points, which I would write out to serve as "memory joggers" to keep me on track. I would use those bullet points to guide me through the actual speech, and if I ever got stuck or on a tangent, I could look at the next bullet point and move toward it. This method worked very well: I knew what I wanted to say, I prepared meticulously, Terry helped with the words and images, and I then spoke from the heart.

There were occasions, however, when I just didn't have the time to go through my normal preparations and practice enough to get to that bullet-point step. In one such case, I asked for a teleprompter so I could read the speech. After all, it was well written and strong; the words were beautifully chosen to articulate the points we wanted to make. I expected to be just as effective reading it as I would have been speaking from notes, maybe even better. At least, that was the theory.

After the speech, I spoke with Jan Hier-King, a member of my executive team, whom I valued highly because I knew I could always count on her to tell me the truth, even when it was a hard truth—and she rarely minced her words. This instance was no exception.

"Jan," I asked, "what did you think?"

"Horrible," Jan said immediately. "I hated it. You delivered the speech pretty well, but we could tell that you were reading it. It didn't come from your heart and it didn't sound like you. You know," she added, "it's about how you make us feel. Your authentic display of passion and emotion energizes us. That's what makes a good speech. This didn't work, Dave."

Jan was right, and I was wrong in thinking the words themselves would be sufficiently compelling. Terry and I had a metaphor for the error: "You got the words, but you didn't get the music." No speech-writer can do that; you have to call it from yourself. If you're lucky, you'll have trusted advisors to help you and remind you, as needed.

Having learned that simply reading a speech is not effective (and can be counterproductive), and having relearned that preparation is essential, I was interested to hear Intel's Renée James describe her strategy for communicating with her people in a compelling way: "I write out what I want to say verbatim, long-hand, very old fashioned. Sometimes I have PowerPoint slides with the high-order concept; usually I memorize key words."

Renée knows exactly where the emphasis needs to lie: "The most important parts of a presentation are beginning high, ending strong, and the key phrases in between. You need to think about the story you want to tell and the things that you want people to do as a result of having heard it." Renée establishes those key points first and writes them down. She likes "to use alliterative words or use repetition in a motivational role." She also looks to "other effective speechmakers, like John F. Kennedy or even President Obama."

Stressing the importance of practice and memorization, she reinforced my experience. "When you are trying to inspire people, the worst thing you can do is just read something. It has to come from your soul. People respond the best in those times when I get up and talk about my belief in what is possible. They don't know about the time I spent writing all this out or the 1,000 times I practiced it. What they hear is my passion and my belief."

Renée also makes the challenges clear. "The emotional connection is really important. And that happens in the first few minutes of a speech. That's why the first three sentences are so critical. I strive not to get super technical or precise in those sentences, because that's when people are still deciding if they are going to listen to you or not." Hers is a good point: we have to move people to listen and pay attention rather than simply be in attendance during our speeches.

"Having a relatively thought-provoking, intellectually stimulating comment right up front helps. I don't mean you should start with a joke or anything like that, just a statement that opens up the dialogue and thought: The world is doing X and here's how you are involved. People respond to the personal and individual—and everyone wants to hear about themselves!"

Renée underscores important concepts here. One is that we need to think seriously about what we want our speech to do, the kind of impact we want it to have, the action we want people to take when they leave the room. This is the heart of the issue: what do we want people to feel, to believe, and to do after they have heard our speech? Are people going to leave the meeting ready to run through the wall and take on the whole world? Or are they going to shake themselves awake and trudge over to the next meeting? If you cannot connect with people, then your ideas—no matter how important and how well thought out—will fall into a black hole.

Even if you think your idea is so good it can sell itself, take a step back and remind yourself that sitting in an audience, sometimes for hours on end, listening to a series of speeches is asking a lot from people who are more used to an active work day. And no matter how well delivered those speeches are, the audience members have work waiting for them. Indeed, whenever you are speaking before a large audience, first consider the question, "Is there some reason why these people might not really pay attention to what I am about to say?" For example, was there a recent article or web post or even a broadly circulated e-mail that stirred things up? If so, acknowledging this right up front can be an effective element of your talk. If you're not aware of any specific issue, then even addressing the length of the meeting can help. Starting with something as simple as, "I know I'm the last person between you and lunch, but in the next 25 minutes I have something to cover that I believe is very important to our future success," can lead you and your audience effortlessly into your topic.

While this discussion has focused on speeches, the same points apply to all of our communication as leaders. A speech is a slice in time, one that warrants extraordinarily thorough preparation. It can have a powerful impact if it resonates, sparks interest, and moves people to action. Speeches are visible and important components of your role as a leader. Successful leaders are conscious of that role in every communication, every interaction, every venue, throughout the organization and beyond. How do you prepare for that?

LEADERSHIP CONNECTION IS A DISCIPLINE

As part of his consulting work and his book *Leading Out Loud*, Terry Pearce created a framework that encourages change leaders to develop a "Personal Leadership Communication Guide" in preparation for and as part of each breakthrough change effort. In that process, you think through every aspect of every communication scenario and write about it, just as you would a journal, except you do it in discrete pieces. Like a journal, you add to it with some regularity. The framework appears at the end of this chapter.

Terry and I have used the Guide in our most successful efforts together. It acts as a reminder in any venue or media, in spontaneous as well as planned situations. Further, working on it sets the stage for your internal process to unfold. Terry and I never use it all and we never read it aloud, but we always use some of it. Once you have thought through the Guide's concepts—competence, trustworthiness, context, the future, personal motivation, and commitment to action—and put them to paper, you will find they come automatically to mind when you need them, as will the personal and relevant stories that support them.

On its own the Guide is not going to transform you into a leader any more than playing scales can make you a great pianist. What counts is what you put into it and grapple with as you consider what has shaped you, what is important to you, and what you see for the future. Here is a chance to ask yourself some fundamental questions about who you are and what you see ahead:

- What accomplishments have made you proud?
- What kinds of changes do you want to be involved with?
- What are you doing?
- Why exactly does this matter to you?
- And why should it matter to others?

When you speak about this, what comes through? Is it just the words, or is the music there as well, resonating in others in ways even they don't understand?

It takes discipline to tackle these questions on your own. In fact, it takes discipline to tackle them even in a structured environment, whether at a training or with a coach. And tackling them as you're simultaneously faced with the crushing pace of business can seem impossible. But do make the time. Allowing yourself to ponder the questions will add depth to your perspective and to your ability to connect with others.

Power Versus Influence

The dichotomy of power and influence plays an important role in leadership. Too many people discuss leadership in terms of power.

In business, we are told we need to become powerful, have power over others. But is that what leaders actually need? I don't want people to take action or behave in certain ways because they fear me, or just because I am their boss. I want people to take certain actions toward the goals we've set—to *feel compelled* to do so—because they too believe that these goals are worth striving for.

At a fundamental level, leaders and followers have to be talking about and focused on the same goals. This speaks to a basic idea about communication: you have to consider others' perspective. It's not about what you say; it's about what they hear. And what you think you are saying can often be very different from what others are hearing.

How best to connect with the people you need to lead? We started on this topic back in Chapter One with the first step of the Stacking the Deck process. In laying the groundwork for breakthrough change, you have to first establish the need and a sense of urgency. Of course, you must have facts that support you, but for people to get drawn in and be convinced of the need for action, they need to believe you. You therefore need to make it personal, to involve people with stories that make the need real. Ginger Graham made the need doubly real by bringing in people whose lives had been saved thanks to intervention by talented invasive cardiologists who implanted her company's stents. Yet even without enthusiastic testimonials from customers, you will find you can connect more effectively by drawing on your life experiences inside and outside of work.

Personal Perspective

Your perspective comes from how you view the world combined with who you are as a person. It is molded by the sum total of your experiences and your beliefs. Becoming a good communicator requires that you uncover your own point of view and that you share it with others. Warren Bennis makes the point most succinctly in his book *On Becoming a Leader*: "Leadership without perspective and point of view isn't leadership—and of course it must be your own perspective, your own point of view. You cannot borrow a point of view any more than you can borrow someone's eyes. It must be authentic, and if it is, it will be original, because you are an original." Describing your point of view can be an intimidating proposition, but authentic leaders understand that it is well worth the effort.

In considering and crafting your speeches and in preparing for all your communications as you work on your Guide, you must ask yourself the following questions: "How much of this am I willing to share with others? How much am I willing to reveal of myself?" Sharing who you are and why you believe what you do can be incredibly inspiring to others. The stories you share are part of what makes you real and gives you believability.

Whenever you mine the personal, you must first decide exactly how personal you want to get. Sharing stories of challenges or failures in your own background can be powerful—if you're willing to reveal them honestly. It can be scary to get up in front of a group of people you need to lead and talk frankly about your mistakes. But it is how you make yourself real to others. I could tell you a dozen stories where I had a lot of success and encountered no major problems, but it is the one story of a total fiasco that will show you I have the ability to admit and analyze mistakes, and learn from them. That one story will do more to establish my credibility than the dozen uneventful tales of triumph.

An added benefit of using stories to establish a connection with people is that in telling these stories you will naturally relive them and feel some of their emotion again. The people you are talking with will see that you are really feeling something, and they will naturally connect with those actual expressions of emotion. This builds the authentic connection you are striving for as a leader. Howard Schultz's story about his speech on returning to Starbucks is a great example of how a leader can cultivate an atmosphere of personal connection in this way.

Howard's commitment to transparency and vulnerability did enormous work in building credibility for him as a leader. In his case, Starbucks' financial situation was dire and being radically honest about the standing of the company also imbued his speeches with a sense of urgency. Finally, Howard's emotional honesty, his willingness to share his fears and pain with the employees, created a sense of camaraderie. They were all in the same boat and the only way to save the company was for everyone to put their oar in.

By committing to transparency and to emotional openness, Howard also indicated certain things about himself as a leader and a person. When you are in charge of a big initiative with many moving parts and lots of people, your behaviors and your attitudes will tell people who you are. People are looking for certain qualities and character traits in their leaders: courage, generosity, humility, integrity, resolve, responsibility. They want to know that you are capable of these personal qualities, and you need to show them, again and again. As leaders we must earn respect for our personal character every day.

Because Howard believed passionately in what he was saying, his authenticity came through naturally. He was putting everything on the line because he believed that the salvation of the company would come from the store managers. If you want to be believable, you have to believe.

Spreading the Message

Communicating to the team and the broader community of employees is not a one-time event. The leader must remain visible and engaged, whatever the circumstances. Dave Barger understands this and acts on his belief that "nothing beats the face-to-face interaction." JetBlue has a major part of the airline market in Boston, and the company is a sponsor of the Boston Marathon. The day after the bombings at the 2013 marathon, he flew to Boston to spend time with JetBlue crew members, customers, and with the authorities. He did so without an agenda, but knowing the importance of being present.

Dave has made sure that an understanding of the importance of presence has cascaded through the leadership team and into the organization. This explains why he and his team don't just tell crew members about the J.D. Power and Associates award they've won for customer satisfaction, nine years running. They "let it fly. We put it on the airplane, introduce it in the galley, in the cockpit." It flies everywhere JetBlue flies, and gets photographed with the crew along the way. In addition, JetBlue internal communications—whether newsletters, blogs, or voicemail—are timed so that they "have a cadence that people can count on." This enables people to trust that information will come to them from inside JetBlue rather than an outside source.

Howard Schultz well understood that one speech, no matter how effective, couldn't turn the tide at Starbucks. So he supported this speech and all his actions with multiple levels of messaging. As he explained, "I also began a series of weekly communications. We laid out a 'Transformational Agenda' that we published for everyone in the company to read. Whether you were a barista working 20 hours a week, a store manager, or an executive, this one sheet of paper would tell you what we were doing, why we were doing it and what your role and responsibilities would be in it. Then, every Sunday at home, I penned a 'Transformational Agenda' update that I released every Monday morning. We had a series of these letters that went out and kept everyone informed." Howard's communications were frequent, well thought out, and well received.

Leaders understand the importance of articulating the objective nature of the change and convincing those around them of the urgency involved; they also understand how critical it is to have that certainty on a gut level. If you don't have faith in the change you're proposing, if you don't genuinely believe that it is the best—or only—course of action, you won't be able to convince others.

In today's world of electronic communication it might seem easier than ever to communicate to your organization. After all, it's pretty straightforward to write an e-mail and hit "send all." Unfortunately, connecting is not that simple.

We earn the right to communicate electronically by the time and energy we invest in communicating personally.

I am not going to suggest you ignore the enormous efficiency and simplicity of electronic communication, but I do caution that you recognize its limits. Electronic communication is a tool for communicating *information*—not for inspiring *passion*. There is simply no replacement for standing in front of people and delivering your message in person, speaking from the heart, and never reading a speech.

Sensing the Music

Human beings are wired to read facial expressions and body language. We read and interpret people's movements and expressions, along with the words they speak, to take in what they are communicating to us. When we are deprived of that additional sensory information, when we don't see the person, don't hear inflections, then we can't hear even a whisper of the music (as Terry and I would say) and we have a much different experience of the very same words. It is all too easy to misinterpret tone and emotion when all we have are the words in print or on screen.

We have all seen many examples of e-mails being read and interpreted far differently than what the author had intended. Particularly when the topics revolve around change and asking people to commit to change—concepts that provoke emotional responses—people need as much context as possible. No matter how precise or well intended, the words alone, particularly when transmitted via e-mail, are dangerously prone to misunderstanding and misinterpretation.

Listening for More

Any discussion of communication must include effective listening. As Ginger Graham told me, "There are lots of reasons why listening isn't easy. When you're elevated to a position of leadership, people don't give you honest, candid, unfiltered feedback. They don't say anything good to you because they fear you'll see that as brownnosing. They won't say anything bad to you because they fear losing their job."

We both knew that this problem increases at the higher levels. Ginger explains, "As an executive, you live in a vacuum away from the truth. We all know that every day in big companies, there are realities about who's performing, not performing, what product's good, what's not good; but they don't ever get said out loud. They wind up as corporate secrets. Breaking that down, creating an environment where everyone, even the CEO, gets and gives open and honest feedback is critical to success." It isn't easy to do and sometimes people need training and practice to get comfortable with feedback.

But even beyond this, it is not easy to simply listen with a fully open mind. We all know people—maybe ourselves—whose lips are pursed as they mentally frame their response before the person speaking has even finished. Does that behavior leave you with a feeling of having been thoughtfully heard? Hardly.

It's all about coming to the conversation curious rather than simply "giving someone their day in court" and moving on to the next issue. If we're truly open to people's ideas, we don't just want them to feel heard: we need them to *be* heard. That means we listen thoughtfully; we ask follow-up questions for clarification, depth, and detail. It requires us to show up with the humility to recognize we don't know all the answers, or even all the questions. It requires us to acknowledge that others have important ideas and thoughts to add to our thinking, even if those include objections to our whole idea. Before leaders can help people move forward toward the new, they must first take the time to hear people's resistance and their concerns.

I cannot overemphasize how truly difficult this is. You must prepare yourself to hear—and to want to hear—upsetting, frustrating, and even counterproductive information. Even if this happens right in the moment when your own sense of urgency is telling you, "There's no time for this!" you must make the time and be fully present and aware. This has never been easy for me. I have often stumbled even though I should know better. But I also know that when I muster the patience to engage in this process and be a more effective listener, I learn things I need to know and I am more effective as a leader. For me this will continue to be a lifelong journey.

Q&A Opportunities

Question and answer sessions also demand effective listening and are a very powerful tool if used properly. When you open a presentation to questions from your audience there is an assumption that the answers you give are unscripted and authentic. The truth is somewhat more nuanced, however. Most speeches and opportunities for interactions have a number of fairly obvious questions that you know will be on people's minds. Will there be layoffs? Will there be benefit cuts? How will this affect the promotional calendar? Will locations be shut down? It's not hard to imagine questions like these coming your way.

You can choose to speak to these issues in your presentation or you can leave them for the Q&A session. The point is that you should be prepared for these questions and the many others that aren't so obvious but might pop up. Good preparation means you have already considered a broad spectrum of possible questions that might come your way and have thought through how you would answer them, perhaps even rehearsed this part of your presentation, just as you rehearsed the speech itself.

These sessions are also a chance to build your culture of open and honest communication. I was once conducting a Q&A session in a town hall meeting of a few thousand employees and someone asked me a particularly challenging question that put me on the spot. The question was phrased along these lines: "I noticed in the proxy that you and other top execs received multimillion dollar bonuses last year. How does this square with the culture of economy and expense control you were just speaking about?"

A hush fell. No doubt some employees thought this employee had just stepped on a career landmine. It instantly seemed as though everyone was watching alertly to see and hear my response. Fortunately this was a variant of a question I had anticipated, so it didn't catch me off guard or put me on the defensive, either in my physical stance or my tone. I paused for a breath and said, "I'm sure many of you must be wondering the same thing, so I thank you for putting this issue on the table and giving me a chance to describe how the board's compensation committee process works. But first, let's give this courageous employee a standing ovation for having the courage to ask a question that was on a lot of people's minds!"

This employee gave me a chance to not only clarify the issue but make a deposit to the culture bank and reinforce the value of honest and open communication that we believed in. Instead, had I been combative or dismissive, I would have undermined our cultural values and ensured that in the future no one would trust me enough to offer their truthful opinion.

Ginger Graham describes a similar instance of using her employees' concerns to develop the company's culture as a whole: "We defined very simple words about what we believed were the cultural attributes for the business, including customer satisfaction, a will to win, and accountable results. We asked the employees to help us define those words and what that behavior would look like. And so we changed our language, our performance appraisals, and our reward system to actually align with these behaviors that we wanted people to adopt."

Ginger had just made some truly groundbreaking innovations in process and product sound easy, and I asked her for some personal background. She didn't miss a beat: "I was raised to believe that you act your way to a better way of being. You don't sit around and say, 'I'd like to be a nice person' or 'Someday I'll be better at collaborating on a team.' Instead, you actually act on those behaviors and as you prac- tice, you get better at them. Eventually that's who you are. Then what you do is who you are, not what you say." Hers seems a very direct path to effective and authentic leadership.

If we are going to demand full commitment from our people, we need to demonstrate it for them. We need to be leaders whose char- acter and plans are worthy of being followed. We need to constantly reiterate what we are doing, why we are doing it, why it matters to us. We need to ask ourselves, as Terry once asked me, "Who are you, what do you want, and why?" These were not meant as rhetorical questions but as existential questions. They were the very foundation for how I needed to communicate as a leader.

———

I was enormously fortunate to have been coached by the best. Terry Pearce's Framework for Personal Leadership Communication Guide©, which follows, provides an objective map so that you can create your own Guide for a subjective experience. If you have completed the action items that were provided at the end of Chapter Three, you might wonder if you need the Guide. The action items presented the more concrete steps of communicating about breakthrough change. When you are leading breakthrough change and the innovations that result (as discussed in the next chapter), those action items will help with the practicalities of moving forward, on track and engaged. The Guide takes your preparation to a much deeper level.

The Guide itself is akin to meditation instructions. You can follow them for life and never reach the state of illumination known as satori. But if you consider the Guide thoughtfully and use it as a tool for your own authentic self-examination, then you will find that you have a strong foundation for every communication situation you encounter. Although the document you create is personal and private, and you will rarely if ever use all of it, the effort you put into constructing it will cue your mind and emotions to enable you to tailor your communications appropriately for your audience. In doing so, think carefully about the impact your words can have, whatever the venue or the format. And remember, as Maya Angelou has often been quoted as saying, "People will forget what you said, people will forget what you did, but people will never forget how you made them feel." That gets to the heart of the issue and is a lesson for leaders at all levels.

The work you put into the Guide will help you approach communication authentically. As Terry explains, the Guide can be thought of as "biography with a purpose." Even if your goal (like mine) is to move forward, which hardly includes taking the time to write an autobiography, you will find the self-reflection involved in creating your personal Guide to be crucial to your ability to connect and inspire. The Guide's purpose is both internal—exploring what is important to you and why—and external, explaining what your group needs to do to arrive at the clear and vibrant future you are proposing. What you write in the process of developing and supplementing the Guide will be "biographical as well as situational" and will become the foundation for your communication. Your Guide will evolve over time as you modify and supplement it with relevant new experiences and material. The work you put into it will enable people to sense your passion and conviction and have a sense of your character.

In considering your personal Guide and writing about your history, your experience, and your conviction for the need to bring about the change, you will demonstrate and make real your trustworthiness as a leader, and as *the* leader for this particular change. Understand that the Guide, as presented here, is simply the bare bones and no substitute for *Leading Out Loud*, in which Terry devotes an entire chapter to each of the four main sections of the Guide. In my opinion, Terry's book should be recommended if not required reading for anyone who aspires to lead. The advice and background it provides is critical to authentic leadership.

FRAMEWORK FOR PERSONAL LEADERSHIP COMMUNICATION GUIDE©

1. Establishing Competence and Building Trustworthiness
   - Competence
     - Clarity of purpose
       Problem
       Specific change advocated
       Evidence of compelling need
       Broad implications; value represented
     - Credentials and vulnerabilities
   - Trustworthiness
     - Displaying empathy
       Expressing gratitude
       Acknowledging resistance
       Finding commonality in purpose
     - Willingness to be known
       Personal motivation, personal value
2. Creating Shared Context
   - History
   - Priority
   - Current reality (include barriers)
   - Reinforcing competence and trust
   - Articulating a broader perspective
3. Declaring and Describing the Future: An Act of Creation . . .
   - Vivid picture, sensory-rich images
   - Stakes (If we do . . . If we don't . . .)
   - Values expressed either way
4. Committing to Action
   - Steps (organizational)
   - Personal commitment, personal action
   - Request for action (specific)

12

Innovation: Ideas and Perspectives

In the world of business and leadership books, few concepts have been more thoroughly analyzed than innovation—and rightfully so, since innovation is both indispensable and inspiring. Initially, innovation often seems to come from a place beyond logic: a bright flash, an "aha! moment." By contrast, incremental changes are safe and generally straightforward; they bring steady improvement—to a point. But often not enough to reset the playing board, to rejigger where competitive advantage resides. Since no truly breakthrough change can come about without innovation in the mix, any discussion of implementing breakthrough change must address the role that innovation plays in the process.

Writing this book has given me the unique opportunity to interview a magnificent collection of world-class innovators, whose perspectives come from a variety of industries, company cultures, and economic environments. Collectively we have well over 200 years of experience (probably closer to 300) in driving breakthrough, disruptive change. This chapter presents a variety of views on the topic and a discussion of our perspectives and experiences as innovation leaders.

To thrive in today's business world and prepare for the future, we can no longer simply pay people to show up and give us their effort; we need to enlist their full engagement, their brains, and their passion. The most valuable assets in our organizations are less about capital or existing products and more about the ability to be creative, to come up with innovative ideas, and to cultivate employee engagement and ownership of the future. We need to encourage new ideas that help our organization succeed, to create the type of atmosphere in which new ideas can flourish, where managed risk is celebrated and where people can see their contributions to shared goals. As Charles Handy, best-selling author and former professor at the London School of Business, has said, "Talented individuals want room to express themselves and space for initiative." The long-term strategic advantage is in having people at all levels believe that they can come up with new ideas to create new products and serve customers better—and that doing so can have long-reaching benefits.

This means people like Mark Phillips, a Schwab call center leader who knew he couldn't wait for headquarters to tell him what to do in the face of a severe Denver snowstorm that threatened to shut down the office completely in 1996. Rather than waiting for advice or snowplows, he anticipated what customers would need, rallied everyone, and used every resource at his disposal to meet that customer need. While we at our San Francisco headquarters were trying to figure out some solutions, Mark's wife, Jackie, was already picking people up in the family's four-wheel-drive vehicle and taking them to the office. While we were trying to figure out how to serve these customers, Mark was already arranging for eight of his people to work out of their homes, to continue phoning customers and serving them. Can you imagine if he had asked corporate whether a noncompany person could take a noncompany vehicle to drive people to work in challenging weather and dangerous driving conditions? The lawyers surely would have said no (and may have needed 36 hours to do so!). Meanwhile, Mark was taking extraordinary action on his own. He took some risks, worked with what he had, delighted customers, and set the tone for his employees.

What would we find in Mark's thought process that encouraged such creativity and gave him the courage to implement his ideas? This question takes us to others, all of which are related to securing our future success. How do we make the most of the combined intelligence of the people in our organizations? How do we keep the intelligence of the organization renewed and productive? What maintenance does the imagination require? In what atmosphere do innovation and employee engagement flourish? These are questions we must hold in mind as we build our culture, reinforce our purpose, and let our employees know how important they are to our future success. These are questions we must ask if we are to truly empower people to work together and bring their best ideas forward; for no one of us can be the source of all the new ideas and innovations we need, big and small.

INNOVATING BY MEETING UNSPOKEN AND UNDISCOVERED NEEDS

The best and most successful companies are adept at meeting needs that don't exist yet—or exist at a low boil in the back of people's minds. Before the iPod existed, no one thought they needed to carry 8,000 songs around in their pocket. Now many of us don't leave home without at least two fully loaded iDevices. And look how the competition has responded with a flurry of new products. Market leadership is fleeting if innovation is not constant. If we are willing to declare a situation "good enough," we lose out on untold opportunities. We must be willing to create a future out of nothing—and keep creating it.

Listen and Learn

Successful innovators and those who strive to innovate are always looking for basic guidelines about where innovation comes from and how to mine those opportunities. For the most part, many of the best and most overlooked insights regarding innovation come from the people on the ground. Ideas come from your front-line employees and, most of all, your customers. This doesn't mean that you should go to your customers expecting a solution to the problem of the moment. Solutions are *your* job. But an important first step in uncovering them is listening to customers. Take the opportunities to listen, and customers will tell you where the problems are that could use your attention. They definitely know what isn't working. They are very good at identifying their unmet needs or the services or products they aren't getting from your business as it currently exists.

Talking with and listening to customers is an excellent—perhaps the best—way of getting the pulse of a business. The foundation of your communication with the customer should be face-to-face meetings; surveys can supplement the knowledge you gain from those more personal meetings. In turn, you need to be sure that your organization's members and its processes are ready to listen to and act on what the customers are telling you.

Pinkberry's Ron Graves says that "there's just no substitute for being out there and talking and seeing and feeling. As the leader of this organization, I see and feel things that others might not. Being on the floor and with customers is essential; I learn so much. It's been so important to me that our head of marketing now works in one of our stores once a week. In most organizations, that's unheard of. Is that a good use of time? Absolutely."

Ron explained how, in just the first month that the head of marketing worked in the store, "the number and depth of insights that she brought back—about how to innovate product, communication, the service model—was staggering." The benefits of this newfound knowledge quickly spread: "It's helping everyone, including the executive team. What has been most gratifying to me is that when I suggested this to the head of marketing, she took it on with vigor. Her eyes have really been opened."

When a project works this well, a smart leader knows to widen its reach. Pinkberry is expanding this initiative: "We're having other people with vital positions in the company, who have customer interaction positions in the company, work in the store. And we're not talking about once a year working the store for a couple hours. We're talking about immersing yourself in the store, operating the point of sale, making product, serving customers. There's no better value. It's amazing to me that more people don't do this."

Ron's enthusiasm was contagious and his story is a wonderful example of a CEO using his power well. A midlevel executive might see the need to do this but be reluctant to do something so novel and unusual. By having the executive team set the benchmark, Ron has ensured that the acceptability of this type of activity will ripple through the organization. Some people argue that CEOs can never be true innovators since they are too disconnected, busy, or both to do the roll-up-your-sleeves work. Yet Ron's experience demonstrates that the CEO can put the processes and procedures in place to ensure that innovation happens.

Ron's company has benefited from consistent efforts to listen to customers and from what employees learn in face-to-face interactions with them in the stores. Similarly, companies can benefit greatly when leaders seek out employees and listen to their opinions and solutions. Sometimes what's needed are simply opportunities for interaction; sometimes it takes the right open-ended questions. What is always required is that leaders actively engage, even when they might want to sit back and relax. One example that came up with a number of leaders are the celebratory events companies hold to honor employees. Leaders have responsibilities in these events that go far beyond introducing award-winning individuals and teams and handing out awards. They need to view these events as opportunities to interact with those being celebrated to learn from them; they also need to initiate conversations with attendees who, with the right question or the right inspiration, might well be the next honorees.

Create Opportunities to Interact

Being out on the floor is clearly helpful, as is creating frequent, regular opportunities for customers to speak with you. Be alert to those possibilities and create new ones when you can; gather information all the time.

When I was at Schwab, I instituted a monthly luncheon designed to gather and share information. We hosted 24 customers and 12 employees at each luncheon, thus ensuring that each customer would receive individualized attention. The employees included a mix of very senior staff and those who led departments or units responsible for services, products, or policies. Customers who shared some important attribute would be invited to the same luncheon. For example, one luncheon's attendees would be new customers from full-service firms with accounts above $250,000; another's would be customers with accounts above $250,000 who just *left* us to go to full-service firms. Or it might be customers who had been with us for more than 10 years but who recently closed their accounts to go to Fidelity. Or a room full of active traders, customers who traded more than 100 times a year. It was the passion behind the customers' words, the look in their eyes, the way they told their stories that gave us the information, perspective, and insight to take meaningful action. Customers were pleased to be heard and to see that we cared about their ideas and how we could improve our services.

Ask Questions

Whether it's lunches, town hall meetings, or more informal interactions, shake people's hands and engage with them. Ask them critical questions: "What is not working for you right now? What are the pluses and the minuses of doing business with us? What are our competitors doing that we don't, and should?" Ask open-ended questions and high-gain questions, both of which provide information and keep the conversation flowing. You don't want yes or no answers; you want answers that provide insight. Keep probing until you gain a new insight. And then follow up. Simple as it sounds, asking questions is one of the largest components of successful innovation.

Complaint letters from customers would cross my desk with some regularity back when I was an executive at Schwab. After reading them to get a feel for customers' concerns, I would send them down to a unit called the "Chairman's Division" where complaints that came to me or to Chuck Schwab were investigated and addressed. Occasionally, I would receive a second letter from the same person, complaining about a lack of response. After this happened a few times, I headed downstairs to ask what was going on.

As I soon learned, the process for investigating these complaints was more labor-intensive than I'd imagined. People had to enter the complaints into the system, call the branch or call center to investigate, and resolve the issue before writing a letter back to the customer. All told, the average time required was about two weeks. The fact that we were getting second letters in some cases was proof that our customers thought the process should be faster. They were right, and this needed to be fixed. So I asked the question, "What would it take to lower that response time?"

The more we looked at the situation, the more we saw places where we could automate and streamline. Here and there, we cut process steps and automated, reducing the wait time from 14 days to 11. Then to 9. Then to 6.

That was pretty good, but it was still in the realm of incremental change and we were interested in a more radical approach. "What about one day?" I asked. "What would it take to get back to customers in one day?" Those questions kicked off an entirely new level of thinking. Now we weren't just focusing on process steps; the problem went deeper. What would we have to change about our business model to have the caliber of customer service that a one-day response would reflect?

At the same time, we were trying to develop a sense of how much these investigations were costing us in time, resources, and labor. Eventually we determined that handling each one of these complaints wound up costing about $200. Meanwhile, 80 percent of our inquiries had to do with problems that involved amounts less than $200. Suddenly the solution was obvious.

From that point on, whenever a customer complaint valued at $200 or less came in, we simply made the customer whole again rather than going through the entire investigation process. As a result, we saved money and time, and the customers were delighted by the advocacy and goodwill we demonstrated with this approach. Until we became aware that our response time was a problem for customers, we hadn't thought to assess our system. But by first raising the small question, "What would it take to lower that response time?" we had looked at the system more closely. Once we did that, we improved—incrementally at first. Then with the bolder question, "What about *one* day?" we found a chance to improve that we wouldn't have discovered if we hadn't challenged the process and ourselves. As for those complaint letters, we continued to attend to them, watching for any larger issues or patterns that would point to future needs or improvements.

Generally, when it comes to questions, bigger is better. After all, the beginning of breakthrough innovation often comes out of asking bold questions. In speaking with customers, after you've laid some groundwork, consider asking questions that might at first appear pie-in-the-sky, or even irrelevant: "What are your hopes and dreams right now? Absent any limits whatsoever, what would you want from our company?" Asking questions such as these helps people look toward the future and think beyond the possible. You need to ask more than just the clients; ask similar questions of your team and your employees. As described in Chapters One and Eight, the questions that Ginger Graham asked of her team at Advanced Cardiovascular Systems and the freedom she gave them to develop the answers resulted in life-saving breakthroughs in the medical device industry. Whatever field you are in, open yourself to possibility and innovation by asking yourself, "If there were no limits, what would I like our business to do?"

At Schwab, we were paying close attention to our mutual fund business in the late 1980s. People were buying fewer and fewer individual stocks (due to the hangover of the market crash in 1987) and customer behavior was trending toward mutual funds. Unfortunately, we didn't have a very big share of the pie and we could see that it was going to hurt us down the road. Instead of asking ourselves, "How can we improve mutual fund sales by 5 percent? Or 10 percent? Or even 20 percent?" we set our sights higher. We asked, "What would we have to do to become one of the *top three distributors* of mutual funds?"

Our first step was to go to the customers. We asked them why they purchased—or didn't purchase—mutual funds through Schwab. Customers informed us that they enjoyed the amazing selection of "no-load" mutual funds that we offered and the convenience of doing business with us, but often resisted buying from us because using our mutual funds service was more expensive than going directly to the funds themselves. If you went to each no-load fund directly, you dealt with many companies, but there was no fee involved. At the time, we were charging the customers a service fee for Schwab's role as a supplier of a broad array of no-load funds from many different fund companies. No other firm provided this service, and it certainly was convenient—but it came with a price. We had a wonderful service, but we were also the most expensive place to invest in no-load funds.

The solution was obvious: we had to become less expensive—indeed, we had to make our service free to customers. And we had to earn revenues from somewhere. The only other viable source of service fees was from the mutual funds themselves. At that time, no-load mutual funds had never paid a brokerage firm for distribution or servicing. Most people in the industry believed we could never convince funds to do this. But we had to find a way, and we did.

Not all of the funds in our marketplace would go with us on this approach, but much to the industry's amazement eight mutual fund firms agreed to, and we launched with 80 funds on our platform. When we had first started growing our mutual funds division, it took us eight years to reach almost $2 billion in assets held at Schwab. In the six months after we implemented this change and stopped charging clients, we just about doubled that figure. As of 2012, the twentieth anniversary of this service, Schwab was offering 4,400 funds from 430 mutual fund companies for a total of $216 billion.

We got there by asking big questions of ourselves and of customers, aiming high, and looking for solutions. Knowing what questions to ask and where you should direct your attention requires a mix of experience and imagination. Challenge yourself, and others, with bold questions. Bold questions—and bold answers—bring breakthrough results.

Aim for "And" Answers—not "Or" Answers

Jim Collins, author of three best-selling business books, has an excellent concept that really gets to the foundation of answering big, bold questions: Always look for the "and" answer, not the "or" answer. Too often, leaders will say things like, "We must choose between great customer service or low prices." Instead, you have to figure out a way to offer both. That kind of open-ended thinking can keep you from being hamstrung by the accepted wisdom about what is and what is not possible, and can open up entirely new avenues for you. It's a concept that is now so well understood that car advertisements build on it, promoting the idea that buyers no longer need to choose between great gas mileage or a fun car, but can have both—in one vehicle.

The topic of "and" answers came up in many of my discussions with innovative leaders. Dave Barger and I spoke about this challenge at length in discussing how JetBlue is able to offer a premium seat *and* give great service *and* value to someone sitting in coach. Howard Schultz spoke of how Starbucks struggled to be efficient and move customers through the line while also finding ways for baristas to engage with customers, look them in the eye, and get to know their preferences so that customers could have their regular drink without having to order. Ron Graves stressed that since the frozen yogurt business is hypercompetitive, Pinkberry would need to provide a premium product, a welcoming store environment, *and* still offer great value. All of these approaches reflect forward-thinking innovations. If you want to innovate, don't fall into the trap of thinking that the status quo is good enough or that it can't be changed. Instead, look for the opportunity.

TYING INNOVATIONS TO VALUES

Leaders understand that success can breed complacency, and that's especially true when it comes to innovation. When you have been successful for a long time, it's hard to resist the temptation to play it safe and focus on incremental improvements. You have an existing technology or distribution system or sales structure or product line. Why bother operating outside of that framework or reinventing what's working? Undertaking something new is difficult, particularly when the benefits of implementing it are unclear or unproven; and even more so when the drawbacks and barriers are obvious.

For example, a new product line may well erode the sales of your existing products. You need to decide whether you are willing to take that kind of risk. However, it's a risk either way. We've all heard stories about companies that resisted adding products because they didn't want to cannibalize their existing sales; ultimately, they leave a gap in the market that can be exploited by a competitor. Is it better to risk eating into your own sales (as Apple did to the iPod in introducing the iPhone, and then to the MacPro with the iPad) or letting your competitors do it?

It's always tough to leave a comfortable present for an uncertain future, and it's not just tough on leadership. One of the best ways to make this process easier is to ground the innovation within your culture. When you talk about what is changing, make time to remind everyone what is not changing as well.

Process, procedure, and product are the elements of a business that most commonly undergo regular changes. In many cases, these are constantly changing in incremental or in bold ways. By contrast, a company's big-picture strategy might change only once every five to ten years; and the company's core mission and purpose rarely change at all. Business students are sometimes surprised to learn that in most businesses and industries, the company's core mission and purpose and even the overarching strategies generally remain stable over time. But there are good reasons for this: these core beliefs ground people and let new and long-term employees know what the company is all about.

When we are describing a new process, procedure, or product, we need to contextualize it alongside the company's core values. Yes, we might say, this new product could chip away at sales for some of our other products, but it is wonderfully consistent with who we are as a company. We should all be comfortable with the idea of this product as an important part of our client proposition. Connecting the new change with the old values makes the change less daunting for everyone (except perhaps the team assigned to drive the sales of the older product, but this is manageable and reasonable to expect).

Further, organizations that embrace the concept of Noble Failure, initially discussed in Chapter Ten, find that innovations flow more freely, that the fear surrounding innovation is defused. Asurion's Steve Ellis mentioned that he'd seen some great examples of this in one of their call centers. "In a recognition day at the end of the month, the woman who runs our call centers highlighted two people who had experimented: one with a new technology tool we had introduced and another one with a new technique for handling a certain type of claim. These experiments hadn't worked, the ideas that they had championed hadn't worked—and still the individuals were spotlighted for their efforts and everyone gave them a standing ovation." Steve was all for it: "These are the kinds of messages that ultimately encourage people to take risks and try new things."

That encouragement can make all the difference. Steve explains how risk "can become paralyzing if it's concentrated on an individual. Standing out there alone will magnify the intensity of that risk and, by definition, the consequences if you should fail. Risk is asymmetrical because people tend to run away when things go wrong and crowd together when things go well. That's just human nature. You'll never get as big a share of the accolades as you will of the blame, and that's scary."

Steve continued, describing a policy that he used at Bain and is using at Asurion to spread the risk: "I want to send the message: Yes, you're accountable for driving and leading the change process—we're taking the risk as a management team, which spreads it out and diminishes its impact a bit." He elaborated, "Lowering the risk for the individual gives people the ability to step up and be more creative and more aggressive than they might otherwise."

How does this make the risk easier on employees? As Steve said, "If we're sharing the risk, the information's flowing frequently, keeping the lines of communication open. As a consequence there are more ways to mitigate and manage the risk over time. If it's a shared risk, people are much more comfortable airing problems before they completely derail a project. By contrast, without risk syndication, if there's some sort of big problem, it's just too tempting for people to try to fix it themselves and avoid blame."

Steve has perfectly described what I think of as the best parts of the Noble Failure concept: it's designed to help leaders and organizations support and encourage innovation and breakthrough changes. And in today's hypercompetitive world, nothing less than courageous leadership and breakthrough changes will do.

BREAKTHROUGHS AHEAD

Sometimes the situation you are confronted with calls for a leap of faith. What if no matter how carefully or creatively you crunch the numbers there is little evidence to prove that your approach will provide the outcome you want with a degree of certainty that would make your CFO smile? What if you see opportunities that others can't yet imagine? These can be the scariest innovations of all—and are also the ones that may have the most potential.

Think of Google purchasing a small smartphone operating system called Android and then giving it away for free. Or Larry Baer's investor team buying the failing San Francisco Giants, knowing they needed a new ballpark—and that voters had rejected four ballpark proposals in the previous years. Neither of these moves had economics that any CFO was going to sign up for. They were enormous and daring leaps of faith.

Similarly challenging are the leaps of faith you must take in your business in responding to threats that you can see but that have barely begun to register in the metrics or in your organization's awareness. While no one can predict the future with any certainty, what is certain is that it will bring new challenges and demands. So you carefully evaluate the path you are on. You know in your gut that the current path won't lead to the success you need. Many around you are telling you to just play it safe, to wait and see if things really do get worse. But you know you can't. You see what your competitors are doing, and your gut, fueled by the knowledge and experience you've acquired over time, is telling you that if you don't move and do something breakthrough, your competitors' positions will, over time—and maybe not much time—erode your own. If you find that you have got to do something bold, then you will. By using the Stacking the Deck process, you can prepare yourself and your team as you step forward into that innovative breakthrough change.

EPILOGUE

Final Comments and Reflections

This book grew out of my role as an educator. Teaching in the Wharton Executive MBA and Executive Education programs made it even more clear to me that real, transformational, challenging, risky, breakthrough change is critically important in today's world and ever more challenging to successfully accomplish. Due largely to rapid technological advances, the business world now moves faster than the world I entered years ago, and is increasingly globalized. The competitors have multiplied and the time frame has shrunk. Regulations and oversight grow more burdensome every day. Now more than ever, we need to understand how breakthrough change happens—and how incredibly hard it is.

As much as I have attempted to lay out a clear process, in the end *Stacking the Deck* is a guidebook, not a cookbook. By using the right equipment, skills, and ingredients in the right order, you can be more or less assured of making a beautiful soufflé every time. But break-through change has a near infinite number of variables, more costs, more people, and more constraints. In fact, breakthrough change is so hard that most people have difficulty imagining, never mind preparing for the demands it will require.

Over the course of my life and my career, I've learned methods and techniques to make the change process easier; more than that, I've learned that it's good for the process to be difficult. This is the crucible where substantial competitive advantage and economic value are created. Do not be discouraged by the difficulties you will face in undertaking breakthrough change. The difficulties are opportunities to challenge yourself, and the rewards will be all the greater for the effort.

Not a single one of the nine steps of the Stacking the Deck process is easy. Recognizing a need to change is hard; assembling a team is hard; piloting is hard. What is easy is getting discouraged and becoming disillusioned. You will assume the difficulties you encounter must be your fault, that you must have "screwed something up" because nothing should be this hard. That's when you'll know you're doing it right. Breakthrough change should be that hard. That is partly why I chose to include so many voices in this book: I wanted to demonstrate to readers that even the most successful change leaders struggle and that even their successful initiatives demand extraordinary effort. Challenges, even failures, aren't always about personal inadequacies; enormous successes can grow out of the most difficult situations.

In selecting leaders to interview, I gravitated toward people who were leading interesting organizations that had undergone big changes. I wanted to speak to them about breakthrough change, both to test the validity of my ideas and to gather a variety of great illustrations of the dark days of any big undertaking. I did not confine my interviews to a certain type of company or industry, or focus only on CEOs. I wanted a cross section of people from companies of different sizes, from different levels in their careers, from different roles within their companies. I wanted to look at change from every angle, continue learning, and see if my concepts held up to that kind of scrutiny. The value of these interviews cannot be measured by the quotes that are included in the text. Each interview was rich with ideas that either validated my process or caused me to rethink or modify my approach in some fashion.

These leaders offered a great wealth of specificity, giving rich, clear examples and highlighting issues about breakthrough change that I hadn't explored in depth before. Step Seven, for example, really benefited from many of the conversations we had about finding a balance between an overly restricted budget and one that doesn't offer enough in the way of measurable commitments. I had thought a lot about the differences between traditional proof of concept pilots and my approach of the stacked proof of concept pilot. But I hadn't really articulated the dichotomy between proof of concept and scalability pilots until these discussions.

As it turned out, even though this book started out as a quest for a better educational tool, the process of writing it became a real education for me. In compiling this information and talking with others, I realized that I'd barely scratched the surface of many of these concepts. Writing forced me to examine my own ideas on a granular level. Similarly, teaching the course had forced me to examine—and reexamine—the principles behind the steps.

I know, and have known for decades, that change is difficult and threatening for people. My experience has taught me the landmines and the importance of recognizing and understanding resistance in order to get past it and get people on board with change. I've been teaching these ideas for years—and sometimes I still need reminders.

Before the first day of class in the Fall 2013 Wharton Executive MBA program, I had thought through a change to the final project I would assign to the students. These students are already out in the business world and are emerging leaders, whose companies have handpicked them and are investing in their education. The students are dealing with real problems in their jobs while fitting in coursework and classes two weekends a month. By the time they get to my course, many of them have had more than their fill of case studies. So rather than going with the final project I'd assigned in previous years, I planned to present them with a real problem, give them access to real data, and have them propose and present their solutions and, most important, their implementation plans and approaches. To me, it seemed like a win on all levels.

The day for our first class arrived and I launched into the course introduction I've been using for years. I then began to explain the new structure we would use for our final assignment, a change to what had originally appeared in the previously distributed syllabus. I sensed some discomfort in the class, but it wasn't as though I was springing a change on them after they'd started work on the final project; that was months away. I explained that instead of yet another case study, their final project would enable them to go in depth with a real problem and, working in teams of five to six students, develop solutions and implementation plans that they would then present to a panel of administrators from the school. I didn't see the enthusiasm I'd hoped for, but these students were new to me and I was new to them. That would come, in time. I knew the assignment was a juicy problem and one in which the administrators were interested and eager for input. The students would have free rein in their proposals and would get valuable experience in developing, presenting, and defending their ideas in the process.

The assignment was this: You have been given the task of reinventing Wharton's MBA program for Wharton San Francisco. Your goals are to grow the enrollment 25 percent without diluting the quality of the students accepted. You need to redesign the program to make it more effective, attractive, well respected, and unique. You must be prepared to deal with all the challenges and constraints common to an educational institution. You and your team will be provided with data from Wharton and from competing schools. After analyzing the data and developing your plan, you will present your recommendations for change and your implementation approach in front of the class and a panel of Wharton administrators.

This was an elective class in leading breakthrough change, and from my perspective this new task provided some real challenges that would mirror what the students would face back at work. A few of the students appeared a bit overwhelmed at the prospect, but I was sure this would turn out to be a significantly better learning experience than the previous, more theoretical project. I knew they would learn a lot and trusted that over the course of the semester they would rise to the task.

What I didn't know then was just how unnerving this change was to many of the students. But soon enough, I was informed that a number of students were actively considering dropping the class on the basis of this change to the final project. And then it hit me: I was so enthused about the new project that I hadn't taken the time to consider the *students'* perspectives. I hadn't explained the purpose behind the change. In preparation for the next class, I returned to my principles of leading breakthrough change, focused on the problem to be solved, and reminded myself of the importance of gathering information. I thought about the signals I had missed and how I might bring the students with me.

I opened the next session by saying I realized I had made big mistakes in skipping over crucial steps and not thoroughly explaining my thinking and my intent with the final project. In assuming the concept would be well received, I had missed the opportunity to thoroughly describe the purpose of our change and the benefits I had envisioned. I said that I was interested in hearing any and all concerns the class might have about the final project. I also committed that after discussing their concerns and hearing my more thorough explanation, the class could decide whether to stay with the new approach or return to the original format, via an anonymous vote. If the class members were not convinced of the value of the new project, we would reinstate the project as it had been in previous years.

This made for a very animated class where almost everyone participated. The vote was nearly unanimous for the new project and the teams took it on enthusiastically. A number of the final presentations were remarkably creative and exciting. The final consensus was that this new project was a more challenging and more immediately useful learning experience for the students. In addition to the experience they gained, the students developed a more realistic appreciation for how long it can take to inspire others to embrace a new, innovative idea and how critical it is to think through and thoroughly describe the practical details for implementation.

As it turns out, the initial concern that some class members had voiced—of having already mentally prepared themselves for the initial project—was just the first layer, not the real issue behind their objections. As we got deeper into the discussion, they voiced apprehensions that more closely reflected how people often see change as a threat. These students were worried about offending the administration and putting themselves on the line with ideas that might be unconventional, groundbreaking, or untried. They were anxious that the new project would take more time, energy, and creativity and that grading would be hard. These are certainly all valid concerns. And as the students came to see, these are concerns that leaders need to be able to face and overcome if they are to aim for anything greater than incremental change. I wish I could say it was all planned, but my initial gaffe of inadequately introducing the change turned out to be a useful part of their learning process—and a powerful reminder for me.

Adaptation is as crucial to survival in the business world as it is in the natural world. It is difficult, daunting, and important work. In today's world, you have two choices: lead with change or be forced to play catch-up. You don't need a specific title or position to lead. You can lead breakthrough change from different parts of the company and from different career levels. Even when the role of driving change does not fall directly on your shoulders, you may get the opportunity to be part of a successful team or to advise the senior person above you. Wherever you are, you can contribute to innovation and progress.

In the right hands, and with the right mind-set, the Stacking the Deck steps can create a more productive and more readily navigated path to breakthrough change. The process itself is less about *what* to think than about *how* to think. It's about learning to anticipate and to analyze logically and carefully; thinking creatively and embracing possibilities; learning what to prioritize, where to concentrate energy, and how to move forward while bringing others along with you.

And there's the key: Leaders bring people along. When a clear process is in place, people get energized; they know where they're going and what to do. But strict adherence to the process alone won't meet with success. Instead, it's the combination of ongoing inspiration—the mark of true leadership—with the structure and discipline of the steps and the assembly of a talented team that creates an enormous advantage for a change effort. It is my deepest hope that the material and suggestions provided in this book will encourage and help you to travel the difficult, worthwhile path to successful breakthrough change and the possibilities of the future.

APPENDIX

Featured Leaders

Larry Baer is the president and CEO of the San Francisco Giants, as well as managing general partner of the ownership group. Larry graduated Phi Beta Kappa from the University of California, Berkeley, received his MBA from Harvard Business School in 1985, and spent nearly a decade in the media and entertainment business, most recently at CBS, before helping assemble the Giants ownership group in 1992. He became the Giants' chief operating officer in 1996, its president in 2007, and its president and CEO in 2010, when the Giants won their first World Series in San Francisco.

Larry has overseen all aspects of the Giants' turnaround effort since 1992, including the rejuvenation of the franchise with the signing of Barry Bonds in 1993; the building of AT&T Park, which opened in 2000; World Championships in 2010 and 2012; and a National League record sellout streak of 270 games and counting.

Larry serves on numerous boards and philanthropic enterprises, including the Boys and Girls Club of America Pacific Region, KQED Inc., and the Bay Area Council, and he cochairs the San Francisco General Hospital Rebuild Campaign with his wife, Pam.

Dave Barger is the CEO of JetBlue airlines. He was part of the founding team in 1998, serving as its president and chief operating officer until becoming CEO in 2007. Dave subsequently also assumed the title of president in 2009. David started in the aviation industry in 1982 with New York Air, moving to Continental Airlines in 1988, where he held a series of senior management positions, including vice president, Newark Hub. Dave was the chair of the FAA's NextGen Aviation Advisory Committee from 2010 to 2012. He serves on the board of Pencil, a nonprofit public education organization. Dave also serves on the board of Airlines for America, A4A, and the board of governors of the International Air Transport Association, IATA.

Dave is no stranger to bold change, having led JetBlue through transformational events, and he continues to look for ways to make JetBlue the leader in creating a better flying experience for its customers. JetBlue, now in its fifteenth year, is a breakthrough airline as a Fortune 500 company growing profitably in an industry that wasn't profitable in its first 100 years.

Michael A. Bell is corporate vice president and general manager of the New Devices Group for Intel Corporation. Mike also co-led the Mobile and Communications Group. Prior to joining Intel in 2010, he was part of the executive management team at Palm Inc. from 2007 to 2010, where he served as senior vice president of product development. Mike was vice president, CPU Software, Macintosh Hardware Division, at Apple Inc., and was with Apple for 16 years. He earned a BA in mechanical engineering from the University of Pennsylvania in 1988.

Mike has been in the middle of the smartphone revolution, having worked on the iPhone and Palm Pre programs. He understands the need to drive change internally in an organization and the challenges in bringing customers along. Some of his success can be credited to the extensive network he has maintained over his career, allowing him to tap the right people for any change initiative.

John Donahoe started his career at Bain & Company in 1985 as an associate consultant and subsequently was the worldwide managing director from 1999 to 2005. John left Bain & Company in 2005 to become the president of eBay's Marketplaces where he helped the business double revenue in just three years. In March 2008, John was named president and CEO of eBay Inc., succeeding Meg Whitman. He currently serves on the board of directors for eBay Inc. and Intel Corp. John earned his BA in economics, graduating Magna Cum Laude, Phi

Beta Kappa, from Dartmouth College, and his MBA from Stanford University Graduate School of Business.

John has led an impressive turnaround at eBay, making some difficult and bold decisions, challenging the tradition and cultural norms of the company and his leadership team. His willingness to make breakthrough change has paid off, resulting in growing eBay's revenues from $8 billion to $14 billion and increasing its stock price over 400 percent during the past five years. John has overseen some major acquisitions, which include StubHub, BML, and Braintree, helping eBay become a global commerce platform and payments leader.

Steve Ellis has served as chief executive officer of Asurion LLC, a provider of consumer technology protection services, since October 2012. In his role as CEO, Steve is responsible for global operations and the formulation and execution of Asurion's global strategy. Prior to Asurion, Steve served as worldwide managing director of Bain & Company, a management consulting firm, from 2005 until 2012, and as managing partner for Bain's West Coast offices from 1999 through 2004. He joined Bain in 1993. Steve's consulting career dates back to 1989 when he cofounded Focus Inc., a strategy consulting firm in Silicon Valley. Steve serves on the board of directors for Asurion, the Bridgespan Group (a nonprofit organization), and Charles Schwab. He is also a frequent guest lecturer at Stanford Business School. He earned his BA in economics and history, with honors, from the University of California, Berkeley, and his MBA from Stanford Graduate School of Business.

Steve has extensive experience in formulating bold change plans and seeing them through. He brings a unique perspective on how people react to change and what leaders must do to bring them along to ensure success.

Ginger Graham is the president and CEO of Two Trees Consulting in Boulder, Colorado, and coaches first-time CEOs in leadership, strategy, board-effectiveness, and organization building. Ginger has a diverse background helping companies navigate big change under heavy regulatory conditions. She is the former president and CEO of Amylin Pharmaceuticals, where she launched two first-in-class human medicines for diabetes, and the former group chairman, Office of the President of Guidant Corporation, a global cardiovascular medical device company. Under her leadership, Guidant launched the world's leading stent platform, was listed in the Fortune 500, and was included in *Industry Week Magazine*'s 100 Best Managed Companies in the World. Her career started at Eli Lilly and Company, where she eventually became president and CEO of Advanced Cardiovascular Systems, a wholly owned subsidiary and the world's leading angioplasty company.

Ginger earned a BS in agricultural economics from the University of Arkansas and holds an MBA with distinction from Harvard University, where she served as faculty in entrepreneurship and wrote for the *Harvard Business Review*. She serves on the boards of directors for Walgreen Co., Genomic Health Inc., Proteus Digital Health, Surefire Medical, Elcelyx Therapeutics, Clovis Oncology Inc., as well as numerous academic and philanthropic advisory boards.

Ron Graves is the CEO of Pinkberry Inc., a company he took over from the founders, completely restructured and restaffed, and then guided to become an international franchise operation. Ron started his career in the United States Air Force, where he was an F-16 fighter pilot and an instructor pilot. Ron has over 20 years of experience working with start-ups, helping them to fine-tune operations, organizational structure, and sales and marketing. Prior to joining Pinkberry, Ron was a general partner at Maveron where he spent eight years investing in early stage companies. He earned a BS from the United States Air Force Academy and an MBA from the Kellogg Graduate School of Management at Northwestern University.

Ron's vast experience investing in and leading start-up and early stage companies lends itself to a unique perspective on how to attack breakthrough change. He is used to highly uncertain business conditions and the need for urgency. One of his favorite leadership tools is to put himself and his leadership team on the front lines, working in the stores, to improve their appreciation for the customer's point of view and the millions of little things that drive customer loyalty.

Debby Hopkins is Citi's chief innovation officer, overseeing client-facing innovation. As CEO of Citi Ventures, Debby is also responsible for building partnerships with venture capitalists, start-ups, corporations, and universities. She has held numerous leadership positions at Citi, including chief operations and technology officer and head of Corporate Strategy, Mergers and Acquisitions. Prior to joining Citi, Debby was the chief financial officer of Lucent Technologies, chief financial officer of Boeing Inc., and the vice president of Finance for General Motors Europe. Previously on the board of directors for DuPont, Debby now serves on the board of directors of Qlik Tech and on the advisory boards of Stanford's Technology Venture Partners program and Riverwood Capital Partners. She also serves on the nonprofit boards of Citizen Schools and the Green Music Center. *Fortune Magazine* has twice named Debby one of the most powerful women in American business, and she has been named multiple times to the Institutional Investors Tech 50 list.

Debby knows the uphill battle of implementing innovation and change and takes extra care to evaluate the impact change has on employees. Debby understands the art of putting together the right team of people to lead change initiatives, a step many leaders overlook.

Renée J. James, president of Intel Corporation, has broad knowledge of the computing industry, developed through leadership positions at Intel and as chairman of Intel's software subsidiaries Havok, McAfee, and Wind River.

During her 25-year career at Intel, Renée has spearheaded strategic expansion into proprietary and open source software and services for applications in security and cloud-based computing, and is leading Intel toward a new leadership position in mobile computing. As executive vice president and general manager of the Software and Services Group, she was responsible for Intel's global software and services strategy, revenue, profit, and product R&D. Previously, she was the director and COO of Intel Online Services, Intel's datacenter services business, on the team working with vendors to port applications to Intel Architecture, and was chief of staff for former Intel

CEO Andy Grove. Renée began her Intel career through the company's acquisition of Bell Technologies. She holds a BA and MBA from the University of Oregon.

Renée is a member of President Obama's National Security Telecommunications Advisory Committee. She is a non-executive director on the Vodafone Group Plc board of directors, a member of the C200, and served as independent director on the VMware Inc. board of directors.

Dick Kovacevich was the CEO of Wells Fargo & Company from 1998 to 2007 and chairman up until 2010. Previously the CEO of Northwest Corp. from 1993 to 1998, he led the merger of Northwest Corp. and Wells Fargo in 1998, taking over as the combined company's CEO. Dick led the growth of Wells Fargo over the next 10 years to be one of the largest financial institutions in the world: today it is the most highly valued financial institution in the world, with a market capitalization of over $250 billion. Dick currently serves as trustee of the San Francisco Symphony and a board member of the San Francisco Museum of Modern Art. He serves as a director of Cargill Incorporated and Theranos Corporation. Dick holds an MBA and a BS and Master's in industrial engineering from Stanford University.

Dick is a firm believer in partitioning projects and focusing on the long-term strategy. He used this technique at Wells Fargo in formulating the long approach to the merger of Northwest and Wells, taking his time in implementing a new technology system and retraining employees to enable the long-term growth.

Terry Pearce is the founder and president of Leadership Communication. As one of the world's leading experts on the topic of leadership communication, Terry counsels individual executives in Fortune 100 companies and is a sought-after speaker. Retired as an adjunct professor at the Haas Graduate School of Business, University of California, Berkeley, Terry has also served as a visiting faculty member at the London Business School. He is a doctoral candidate at Pacifica Graduate Institute, studying Comparative Mythology and Depth Psychology. Terry is the author of *Leading Out*

Loud: A Guide for Engaging Others in Creating the Future and coauthor with David Pottruck of *Clicks and Mortar: Passion-Driven Growth in an Internet-Driven World*. Terry's influence and perspective can be found throughout *Stacking the Deck*, particularly in the leadership communication chapter.

Prior to founding Leadership Communication, Terry spent 17 years as a manager and executive with IBM. He is a former fellow and senior vice president of Executive Communication for Charles Schwab & Co. Terry serves as a board member at Center Point and the Pacifica Graduate Institute, and was chairman of the board of the National Endowment for Financial Education. He is a founding director of the Partnership for a Drug-Free California and a former director of the Healthy Cities Project at the Institute for the Study of Social Change.

Howard Schultz is chairman, president, and chief executive officer of Starbucks. Howard moved to Seattle from his native New York and joined the company in 1982 as director of operations and marketing when Starbucks had only four stores. Today Starbucks has 20,000-plus stores in 64 countries, employs over 200,000 partners (employees), and serves more than 70 million customers each week.

Howard has led a transformation of the company, bringing the company to sustainable, profitable growth with a renewed focus on Starbucks coffee heritage, innovation, and the customer experience. He has been recognized extensively for his passion, leadership, and efforts to strengthen communities, with honors including the 2013 Kellogg Award for Distinguished Leadership at Northwestern University, for his commitment to employees and communities, and being named *Fortune*'s 2011 Businessperson of the Year for delivering record financial returns for the company while leading an effort to spur job creation in the United States. He is the best-selling author of *Onward: How Starbucks Fought for Its Life without Losing Its Soul* (2011) and *Pour Your Heart Into It* (1997).

ACKNOWLEDGMENTS

Writing this book was much, much harder than I expected and more satisfying than I could have imagined. Just as with the steps of leading breakthrough change that are laid out in *Stacking the Deck*, one of the first things I needed to do was to get my own team involved.

From the beginning, Michael Levin and his team at Business Ghost were immensely helpful in combining my fuzzy lecture transcripts, class materials, and the ideas and wishes in my head into a draft manuscript, which then became the foundation of this work.

A huge thank-you to my former student and new friend Nate Jewell, who started working with me as an independent study project and who continued assisting me well after his graduation from the Wharton Executive MBA program. His involvement and support throughout cannot be overestimated. He joined me in the interviews, provided a sounding board, worked on crafting the action items, and deserves huge credit for helping take this from idea to reality.

I feel very lucky to have been able to include the voices of Larry Baer, David Barger, Michael Bell, John Donahoe, Steve Ellis, Ginger Graham, Ron Graves, Debby Hopkins, Renée James, Dick Kovacevich, and Howard Schultz, all of whom graciously agreed to be interviewed. These are not individuals who typically meet with authors, and their amazing stories and well-honed insights are not usually available to students or the general public. Thank you for sharing your experiences and knowledge and helping me expand, solidify, and occasionally reconsider my thoughts in the process. I'm honored to be in your company.

The contributions that my colleague Terry Pearce has made began long before I even contemplated writing about breakthrough change. He taught me the importance of authentic leadership communication and guided me along that journey—first as my leadership communication coach for many years and then as a long-standing friend. His book *Leading Out Loud* has a key role in all of my classes, and he has graciously provided the foundation concepts for this book's chapter on leadership communication. In addition to offering his encouragement and suggestions for making this book better, he steered me to Jan Hunter, who as developmental editor pushed me to take the book to the next level. I'm grateful for her editing guidance, clarity, and general counsel. Her contributions exceeded every expectation I had of what an editor would deliver. She didn't just edit the book; she helped me rethink it.

Lindy Muff somehow keeps me on track, on time, and in the right place as I juggle my responsibilities on boards and in my businesses.

I am perpetually grateful to Colleen Bagan, my tireless business partner, who somehow stays on top of everything at Red Eagle, all our portfolio companies, and the myriad responsibilities that pull me in multiple directions simultaneously. Somehow she graciously ensures that everything that needs to get done does. Fortunately, the book made it onto her list.

Since I firmly believe that multiple brains are better than one, I naturally wanted to get as many smart people to weigh in on my manuscript as possible. Often, this meant multiple rounds of edits to evaluate and incorporate the suggestions that came in—and it was absolutely worth it. A big thank-you to Jennifer Povlitz and my other former students, my many colleagues, and my adult children who read the manuscript and offered me their suggestions.

A huge thank-you to my editorial team at Jossey-Bass: John Maas, Christine Moore, Mark Karmendy, Jeff Wyneken, and Karen Murphy, senior editor at Jossey-Bass, who contributed great talent and ideas to this project.

And finally a thank-you to Emily Scott Pottruck, who has been an important part of the process and who encouraged me from the beginning to truly own this book and pour myself into its writing. I might have settled for a lesser book if not for her encouragement.

We've had a great team and I'm grateful to all of you.

ABOUT THE AUTHOR

David S. Pottruck is the chairman of HighTower Advisors, a $25 billion wealth management firm that he helped launch in 2008. He serves on the board of directors of Intel Corporation, where he is a member of the Executive Committee, chairman of the Compensation Committee, and chairman of the Retirement Plan Investment Committee. In addition, he is on the board of directors of several early-stage companies, including CorpU, a twenty-first-century leadership development organization, where he is chairman. Dave was formerly a trustee of the University of Pennsylvania and chair of the San Francisco Committee on Jobs.

Dave joined The Charles Schwab Corporation in 1984 as executive vice president of marketing and led its innovative direct response advertising campaigns. Under his marketing leadership from 1984 to 1987, when the company went public, Schwab's revenues tripled in size. He became Schwab's president in 1992, co-CEO with Chuck Schwab in 1998, and CEO in 2002. During this period, Dave and Chuck worked shoulder to shoulder, together focusing on leading the company, with little attention to their respective titles. Over Dave's

20-year tenure at Schwab, the company's assets in custody grew from $5 billion to over $1 trillion and the equity value of Schwab grew from roughly $50 million to approximately $16 billion.

During Dave's leadership, Schwab refocused its business model entirely on the Internet, a radically transformative move that drove the company's explosive growth. Schwab also led a reinvention of the no-load mutual fund industry with the introduction of the no-fee "mutual fund supermarket" concept, and introduced the RIA servicing business; both innovations are now cornerstones of the discount brokerage industry.

Dave is the coauthor with Terry Pearce of *Clicks and Mortar: Passion Driven Growth in an Internet Driven World*. A top-ten best seller in *BusinessWeek* and on Amazon, *Clicks and Mortar* has been translated into six languages and was on the best seller list in Germany.

He is a senior fellow and adjunct faculty member at the Wharton School's Center for Leadership and Change Management. In 2010 and again in 2012, he received Wharton San Francisco's Outstanding Teaching Award for his course focused on leading breakthrough change. Dave has taught change leadership to hundreds of executives from around the world via programs tailored for specific corporations and in courses offered online through CorpU.

Dave has received accolades and recognition from numerous organizations and publications. He has been named one of the "Top 15 CEOs" by *Worth*; "CEO of the Year" by *Information Week*; "Executive of the Year" by the *San Francisco Business Times*; and "CEO of the Year" by Morningstar. He was named by *Smart Money* as one of the three most influential executives in the world of investing and by *Institutional Investor* as the number one most influential executive in the world of online finance.

In 1999 he was appointed by Congress and then-President Clinton to serve as one of 19 commissioners on the Advisory Commission on Electronic Commerce, which was tasked with producing recommendations on electronic commerce and tax policy, arguably one of the most important policy initiatives of the Information Age.

Dave graduated with a BA from the University of Pennsylvania, and earned his MBA with honors from Wharton. A native of New York, Dave now resides in San Francisco.

INDEX

A

Accountability, 43
Adaptation, 212
Advanced Cardiovascular Systems, 17, 126–128
"And" answers, 202–203
Apple Newton, 167
Asking questions, 199–202
Assessments, 74–75
  for action, 78
  for breakthrough change, 76–78
  for future needs, 116–117
  initial assessments, 75–76
Assumptions
  testing, 141–143
Attitude, 33, 34. *See also* toxic people
Authentic leadership communication, 171–173

B

Baer, Larry, 18–19, 206
  bio, 214
  on demand yield pricing, 140–141
  on finding tangible ways to test concepts and share vision, 53
Barger, Dave, 47–49
  on "and" answers, 203
  bio, 214–215

on face-to-face interaction, 185–186
  on rules of engagement, 130
Barger, Mike, 47–49
Barriers to success, 58–59
  combination of problems, 63–64
  missing skills, 60–61
  resistance to change, 59–60
  rigid processes and procedures, 61–62
  unyielding corporate culture, 62–63. *See also* Bermuda Quadrangle
Being fully present, 178–181
Bell, Michael A.
  bio, 215
  on interim successes and celebrations, 95–96
  on recruiting talent, 123–125
  on re-evaluating the team, 129
Bennis, Warren, 183–184
Bermuda Quadrangle, 58–59
  mapping, 59–63. *See also* barriers to success
Big data, 103–105
Bleeding edge, 166–167
Blue-sky thinking, 49, 74

Breakthrough change
    anticipating and managing risks,
        165–169
    anticipating fear of change, 22–23
    defined, 1–2
    going slow to go fast, 160–162
    leading, 11–12
    and leaps of faith, 205–206
    negotiating terms of a breakthrough
        change initiative, 158–160
    noble failures, 163–165
    risk of failure, 162–169
    role of passion in, 52–53
    and Stacking the Deck, 5
    underscoring the urgency of, 25. *See
        also* change; resistance to change
Business stretch, 167

C

Cabane, Olivia Fox, 24
Capital and other resources, 80–83
Celebrations, 90–92
Change, 1–2
    anticipating fear of, 22–23
    knowing the need for change, 18–19
    underscoring the urgency of, 25. *See
        also* breakthrough change;
        resistance to change
The Charisma Myth (Cabane), 24
Charles Schwab, 8–9, 10
    asking questions, 199–200, 201–202
    clarifying the vision, 50–51
    corporate culture vs. sales, 20–22
    creating opportunities to interact,
        198–199
    and diversity, 118
    noble failures, 163–164
    online/offline hybrid service, 26–28
    recruiting internally, 120
Citi
    stage-gated processes for funding
        innovation projects, 81
Clarifying the vision, 50–51
Clicks and Mortar (Pottruck and
    Pearce), 173
Coghlan, John, 120
Collins, Jim, 91, 202
Commitment, 42–43

Communicating the message, 46–47
    clarifying the vision, 50–51
    strengthening the leadership team
        with constructive debate, 51–52
Communicating to inspire, 170–171
    authentic leadership
        communication, 171–173
    being fully present, 178–181
    engaging with stories, 176–178
    making values visible, 173–175
Complaint letters, 199–200
Conflicts
    facing, 40
    preparing for, 26–29
Connecting to inspire, 181–182
    listening, 187–188
    personal perspective, 183–185
    power vs. influence, 182–183
    Q&A opportunities, 188–190
    spreading the message, 185–187
    using context to avoid
        misunderstanding, 187
Conviction
    leading with, 155–158
Cook, Scott, 162
Corporate culture, 16
    creating a safe environment for
        dialogue, 40
    cultural adaptation, 33–35
    unyielding, 62–63
    using employee concerns to develop
        company culture, 190
Creating the future, 49–50
    clarifying the vision, 50–51
Crossing the Chasm (Moore), 161–162
Cultural adaptation, 33–35. *See also*
    corporate culture
Cultural inertia, 90
Culture of Accountability, 99
Customer-facing change innovation,
    92–93
Customers
    turning to, 92–94

D

Davis, Ernest, 103
Deadlines, 80
Deliverables, 79

Demand yield pricing, 140–141
Diversity, 117–118
Donahoe, John
    bio, 215–216
    on convincing leadership to make
        changes, 28
    on lagging indicators, 108
    on the need for assessment and
        making a plan for the future,
        82–83
    on recruiting internally, 120–122
    on resistance and entrenched
        company culture, 63–64
Dowden, Edward, 163
Downsizing, 68
Dream team, 117
    diversity, 117–118
    drawing a team to you, 123–125
    maintaining the team through the
        project, 167–168
    rebalancing and revamping,
        129–131
    track records, 118–119
    unifying and empowering, 126–128.
        See also leadership teams
Dysfunctions that can destroy
    a team, 38

E
Early adopters, 161–162
Early majority, 162
EBay, 28, 63–64, 82–83
    recruiting internally, 120–122
Ellis, Steve
    on big data, 103–104
    bio, 216
    on evaluating and implementing
        pilot projects, 145–146
    on the "five percent", 138
    on leading with conviction,
        155–158
    on noble failures, 204–205
    on pilot projects, 136
    on resistance to change, 59–60
    on scalability pilots, 144–145
Empowering a team, 126–128
Engaging with stories, 176–178

Erosion of competitive position, 18
Expertise, 4

F
Failure, 4
    noble failures, 163–165
    risk of, 162–169
Fear
    anticipating, 22–23
    understanding and untangling fear
        responses, 23–25
The Five Dysfunctions of a Team
    (Lencioni), 38
Focusing the leadership team, 40–42
Future. See creating the future

G
Giuliani, Rudy, 85–86
Goals, 79
Going slow to go fast, 160–162
Google, 206
Graham, Ginger, 16–17, 126–128
    bio, 216–217
    on communication, 170
    on listening, 187–188
    on using employee concerns to
        develop company culture, 190
Graves, Ron
    on "and" answers, 203
    bio, 217
    on initial assessments, 75–76
    on listening, 197–198
Great by Choice (Collins), 91

H
Handy, Charles, 195
HDWGT. See how do we get there
    (HDWGT)
Heat maps, 105
Hier-King, Jan, 179
HighTower, 129, 143
Hopkins, Debby
    on assessment for breakthrough
        change, 77
    bio, 218
    on breaking things up into a phased
        approach, 89
    on communication, 170

Hopkins, Debby (*continued*)
    on developing a financial plan for
      breakthrough change, 81
    on innovating, 41–42
    on passion, 128
    on understanding people's
      perspectives, 24
    on what is measured, 101–102
Hornthal, Jim
    on big data analytics, 104–105
How do we get there (HDWGT), 78

I

Influence vs. power, 182–183
Innovation, 29, 194–196
    asking questions, 199–202
    creating opportunities to interact,
      198–199
    listening and learning, 196–198
    tying to values, 203–205. *See also*
      interacting to innovate
Intel
    downsizing, 68
    interim successes and celebrations,
      95–96
    recruiting, 123–125
Interacting to innovate
    aiming for "and" not "or" answers,
      202–203
    asking questions, 199–202
    creating opportunities to interact,
      198–199
    listening and learning, 196–198. *See*
      also innovation
Interim successes
    building in celebrations, 90–92
    buying more time with, 94–96
    planning for, 89–90
    turning to the customer, 92–94
Internet of things, 146–147
Intuit, 162
Investment size, 168–169

J

James, Renée
    on assessments, 77–78
    on belief in a mission, 52–53
    bio, 218–219

    on communication, 179–180
    on the connection between the
      change and the mission, 17–18
    on the need to stay energized, 91
    on people's connection to the
      mission, 84
    on researching for the future, 146
    using evidence of success to
      convince, 90
JetBlue, 47–49, 74–75, 185–186, 203
    radical common sense, 48–49
    on rules of engagement, 130

K

Key results
    knowing, 99–101
Kotter, John, 2
Kovacevich, Dick, 73–74
    bio, 219
    on celebrating people's
      accomplishments, 113
    on evaluating and implementing
      pilot projects, 145

L

La Russa, Tony, Jr., 130–131
Lagging indicators, 107–109
Late majority, 162
Leaders interviewed, 208–209
Leadership
    leading with conviction, 155–158
    vs. management, 131
Leadership teams, 31–32
    bringing outside experience in,
      33–35
    building trust, 38–39
    dysfunctions that can destroy a
      team, 38
    facing conflict, 40
    finding and nurturing the pioneers,
      32–36
    focusing, 40–42
    four elements to look for in team
      members, 32–33
    gauging your ability to manage the
      team, 37–38
    reconfiguring as needed, 36
    strengthening with constructive
      debate, 51–52

taking steps to unify the team,
36–43. *See also* dream team
Leading breakthrough change, 11–12
Leading Change (Kotter), 2
Leading indicators, 105–108
Leading Out Loud (Pearce), 15, 173, 192
Leaps of faith, 205–206
Lencioni, Patrick, 38
Listening, 187–188
    and learning, 196–198
Loss of compelling opportunity
    to grow, 18

M
Magowan, Peter, 18–19
Management
    keeping management on board, 168
    vs. leadership, 131
Marcus, Gary, 103
Matteson, Fred, 93–94
Measuring. *See* metrics
Metrics
    big data, 103–105
    knowing your key results, 99–101
    lagging indicators, 107–109
    leading indicators, 105–108
    sharing results, 111–114
    vintage and ratio analysis, 109–110
    what you're measuring, 101–102
Mission
    linking purpose and, 16–18
    people's connection to, 84
Momentum, 49–50
Money, 29
Moore, Geoffrey, 161–162
Myers-Briggs assessments, 41

N
Need
    knowing, 18–19
Negotiating terms of a breakthrough
    change initiative, 158–160
Nicolls, Marcus, 99–101
9/11 Attacks, 85–86
Noble failures, 163–165

O
On Becoming a Leader (Bennis),
    183–184

Onward (Schultz), 92
Optimized proof of concept pilot. *See*
    stacked proof of concept pilot
"Or" answers, 202–203
Outside experts, 68

P
Partners in Leadership Workplace
    Accountability Study, 100
Passion, showing, 52–53
Pearce, Terry, 15, 37, 84, 171–173,
    178–179
    bio, 219–220
    on personal leadership
        communication guides, 181–182,
        190–192
People, 29
    and the mission, 84
Personal Leadership Communication
    Guide, 181–182, 190–192
Perspectives
    anticipating fear of change, 22–23
    personal perspective, 183–185
    preparing for resistance and
        conflicts, 26–29
    underscoring the urgency, 25
    understanding and untangling fear
        responses, 23–25
    understanding the audience's
        perspective, 20–22
Phillips, Mark, 195
Pilot projects, 134–135
    evaluation and implementation,
        145–146
    gaining advocates, 142–143
    as a part of change initiatives,
        135–136
    researching for the future,
        146–147
    scalability pilots, 144–145
    stacked proof of concept pilot,
        137–140
    testing assumptions, 141–143
    testing before transplanting a
        concept, 140–141
    traditional proof of concept pilot
        implementation, 136–137
Pinkberry, 75–76, 197–198, 203

Planning and budgeting, 72–74
  capital and other resources, 80–83
  deadlines, 80
  goals and deliverables, 79
  people, 84
  tasks, 79–80. *See also* assessments
Planning for interim successes, 89–90
  building in celebrations, 90–92
  turning to the customer, 92–94
Planning for risks, 84–86
Planning for the unexpected, 64–65
  examining potential resistance,
    65–68
  using outside experts to sharpen the
    focus, 68
Power vs. influence, 182–183
Processes
  overly rigid processes and
    procedures, 61–62
Progress, 15
Progress reports, 90
  sharing results, 111–114
Proof of concept pilots, 136–137. *See
  also* pilot projects
Proulx, Tom, 162
Purpose
  linking to the mission, 16–18

Q

Q&A opportunities, 188–190
Quality of the planning effort, 169
Quicken, 162

R

Radical common sense, 48–49
Ratio analysis, 110
Recruiting
  becoming a magnet for talent,
    122–126
  inside your organization, 120–122
  outside your network, 125–126
  skill gaps, 122. *See also* dream team
Resistance to change, 59–60
  examining potential resistance,
    65–68
  preparing for, 26–29
Risks
  anticipating and managing, 165–169

business stretch, 167
of failure, 162–169
investment size, 168–169
keeping management on board, 168
maintaining the team through the
  project, 167–168
planning for, 84–86
quality of the planning effort, 169
scope creep, 166
technological stretch, 166–167
vs. uncertainties, 65–66
Rules of engagement, 130

S

San Francisco Giants, 18–19, 140–141,
  206
Sawi, Beth, 120
Scalability pilots, 144–145. *See also*
  pilot projects
Schultz, Howard
  on "and" answers, 203
  bio, 220
  on connecting with people, 184–185
  on convincing everyone to get on
    board, 91–93
  on the drive to innovate, 29
  on failing fast, 139
  on getting everyone on board, 32
  on making values visible, 173–175,
    176
  on multiple levels of messaging, 186
  on pilot projects, 135
  on rebalancing and revamping the
    team, 130–131
Schwab, Chuck, 8–9
Scope creep, 166
Seip, Tom, 120
Sharing results, 111–114. *See also*
  celebrations
Skills
  gauging the skills needed, 76
  missing, 60–61
  skill gaps, 122
Sneakerware, 147
Stacked proof of concept pilot,
  137–140
  testing assumptions, 141–143. *See
    also* pilot projects

Stacking the Deck process, 3–5, 156,
    208, 212
    navigating and sequencing the nine
        steps, 153–155
    steps, 5–6
Stage-gated processes, 81
Starbucks, 28–29, 91–93, 130–131,
    203
Stories
    engaging with, 176–178
Strategic plans, 73
    and budgeting, 74
Stupski, Larry, 9, 21, 171
Style of Influence, 41

T
Tasks, 79–80
Team dynamics, 41–42
Team Insights, 42
Team-building, 39
Teams. *See* dream team; leadership
    teams
Technological stretch, 166–167
Testing assumptions, 141–143
Three-to-five-year plans. *See* strategic
    plans
Time, 29
Tools
    Myers-Briggs assessments, 41
    Style of Influence, 41
    Team Insights, 42
Toxic people, 35. *See also* attitude

Track records, 118–119
Trust, building, 38–39
Twenty-mile march, 91

U
Uncertainties vs. risks, 65–66
Unifying a team, 126–128
Unknown unknowns, 86
Urgency, 25

V
Values
    making values visible, 173–175
Variable pricing, 140–141
Vintage analysis, 109–110
Vision
    clarifying, 50–51

W
Weissbluth, Elliot, 143
Wells Fargo
    strategic plan, 73–74
Wharton Executive MBA and
        Executive Education programs,
        207, 209–212
Where we are (WWA), 76
Where we want to be (WWWTB),
    76–78
Word clouds, 105
Work styles, 41
WWA. *See* where we are (WWA)
WWWTB. *See* where we want to be
    (WWWTB)